W9-BOD-663

Revised Updated Edition

Job Résumés

How to Write Them
How to Present Them
Preparing for Interviews
(Includes a list of 100 questions most often
asked by the Interviewer)

J. I. Biegeleisen

A PERIGEE BOOK

PERIGEE BOOKS
ARE PUBLISHED BY
THE BERKLEY PUBLISHING GROUP
200 MADISON AVENUE
NEW YORK, NY 10016

COPYRIGHT © 1991, 1982, 1976, 1969 BY J.I. BIEGELEISEN
ALL RIGHTS RESERVED. THIS BOOK, OR PARTS THEREOF,
MAY NOT BE REPRODUCED IN ANY FORM WITHOUT PERMISSION.
PUBLISHED SIMULTANEOUSLY IN CANADA
FIRST PERIGEE EDITION, 1983
ONE PREVIOUS GROSSET & DUNLAP PRINTING

LIBRARY OF CONGRESS CATALOGING-IN-PUBLICATION DATA
BIEGELEISEN, J. I. (JACOB ISRAEL), DATE
  JOB RÉSUMÉS : HOW TO WRITE THEM, HOW TO PRESENT THEM, PREPARING
FOR INTERVIEWS (INCLUDES A LIST OF 100 QUESTIONS MOST OFTEN ASKED BY
THE INTERVIEWER) / J.I. BIEGELEISEN. — REV. UPDATED ED.
    P.   CM.
  INCLUDES BIBLIOGRAPHICAL REFERENCES.
  ISBN 0-399-51692-1
  1. RÉSUMÉS (EMPLOYMENT)   2. EMPLOYMENT INTERVIEWING.   I. TITLE.
HF5383.B46 1991   91-4752 CIP
650.14—DC20
PRINTED IN THE UNITED STATES OF AMERICA
      9   10   11   12   13   14   15

THIS BOOK IS PRINTED ON ACID-FREE PAPER.
                ∞

Contents

Résumé-Selector Index   4
An alphabetical index of sample résumés, keyed by page number to correspond to exact, as well as to equivalent and related, occupational titles.

About This Book   7
Notes on special features of this book that distinguish it from others in the field.

SECTION 1 Compiling Data for Your Job Résumé   9
What Purpose Does a Résumé Serve?   9
What Points of Information Should a Résumé Include?   11
Format and Physical Appearance of Job Résumés   16
The Language of Job Résumés   17
Letters—Transmittal and "Broadcast"   20
Questions and Answers Relating to Résumé Preparation   21
Summary of Work Experience   25
Summary of Educational Background   26
Broadcast Letter Example   27
Cover Letter Examples   28

SECTION 2 Portfolio of Sample Résumés   31
Résumé Formats and Layouts   31
Self-Appraisal Personality Rating Scale   100

SECTION 3 The Job Interview   101
Meeting Your Prospective Employer   101
100 Questions Most Frequently Asked by the Interviewer   101
Questions You May Ask the Interviewer   104
Interview Pitfalls and How to Avoid Them   105
Annotated Bibliography and Other Source Materials   110

Résumé-Selector Index

Accountant 42-43
  Auditor
  Certified Public Accountant
  Controller
  Credit Manager
  Financial Executive
  Treasurer

Administrative Assistant 40
  Administration and Management
  Executive Assistant
  Executive Secretary

Advertising and Merchandising Director 64-65
  Advertising Director
  Merchandising Specialist
  Promotional Director

Architect 98
  Building Engineer

Art Director 59
  Advertising Artist
  Artist
  Designer
  Director of Advertising
  Free-Lance Designer
  Handicapped Worker
  Illustrator

Audiovisual Technical Consultant 96-97
  Communications Consultant
  Consultant (Audiovisual)
  Free-lance Work
  Part-time Work

Bank Manager 55
  Financial Manager
  International Banking Manager

Broadcaster 86
  Announcer
  Entry Position

Radio Broadcaster
Sports Broadcaster
TV Broadcaster

Calligrapher 57
  Artist
  Free-lance Artist
  Handicapped Worker
  Homebound
  Self-employed

Career Change 37
  Homemaker Returning to Work
  Librarian
  Library Research Worker
  Part-time Work
  Retiree Going Back to Work

Chemical Engineer 74-75
  Business Analyst
  Product Engineer
  Sales Manager

Chemist 89
  Analytical Chemist
  Physical Chemist
  Scientist

Computer Programmer 68-69

Data Processor 66

Dental Hygienist 83
  Dental Assistant
  Dietician
  Nurse
  X-ray Technician

Display Designer 62-63
  Artist
  Display Design Consultant
  Exhibit Designer
  Layout Artist
  Letterer

Point-of-Purchase Designer
Window Display Artist

Econometrician 90-91
  Economist
  Market Analyst
  Operations Analyst
  Statistician

Editor 58

Electronics Engineer 67
  Computer Electronics Engineer

Engineering Administrator 70-71
  Civil Engineer
  Structural Engineer

Fashion Model 77
  Model

Financial Analyst 95
  Business Manager
  Overseas Employment

Geologist 85
  Earth Scientist
  Energy Resource Specialist
  Stratigrapher

Industrial Manager 56
  Business Manager
  Office Manager
  Works Manager

Industrial Relations Specialist 36

Journalist/Photographer 60-61
  Freelance Writer

Lawyer 88
  New Graduate
  Recent Graduate

Marketing Management Trainee 54
  Entry Job
  New Graduate
  Recent Graduate

Marketing/Sales Manager 52-53
  Marketing Manager
  Product Development Consultant
  Promotion Specialist
  Sales Manager

Mechanical Engineer 73
  Sales Engineer

Military Returnee 36
  Returning to Work
  Second Career

Paralegal 38
  Administrative Assistant
  Legal Secretary
  Secretary

Part-time Employment 33
  After-school Work
  Copy Boy/Girl
  Editorial Assistant
  Free-lance
  Journalist
  Reportorial Journalist

Personnel Manager 44-45
  Director of Employment
  Employment Manager
  Personnel Interviewer
  Supervisor of Personnel

Photocompositor 99
  Computer Printing Technician
  Graphic Arts Technician
  Printing Technician
  Typographer

Physician 94
  Public Health Service

Physiologist 92-93
  Biochemist
  Medical Research Assistant
  Medical Researcher
  Scientist

Printing Technician 50-51
   Graphic Arts Specialist
   Printer
   Printing Supervisor
   Production Department Manager

Private Investigator 80
   Claims Adjustor
   Detective
   Police Officer
   Security Officer
   Surveillance

Purchasing Director 48-49
   Buyer
   Purchasing Agent

Receptionist 41
   Gal/Guy Friday
   Secretary

Recreation Leader 82
   Camp Counselor
   Playground Director

School Principal 87
   Dean
   Educator
   Headmaster
   School Administrator
   Teacher

Secretary-Bookkeeper 39
   Clerical Worker
   Gal/Guy Friday
   Receptionist
   Typist

Social Worker 84
   Case Worker
   Guidance Counselor
   Psychologist

Systems Analyst/Mathematician 72
   Data Analyst
   Mathematician
   Physicist (Applied)
   Programmer
   Statistician

Therapist 81
   Case Worker
   Music Therapist
   Nursery Counselor
   Occupational Therapist
   Recreational Therapist
   Rehabilitation Specialist
   Social Worker

Tool and Die Maker 76
   Engineer (Tool and Die)
   Machine Shop Technician

Traffic Manager 46-47
   Foreign Branch Representative
   Import-Export Business Manager
   Overseas Traffic Manager
   Sales and Marketing
   Shipping Expeditor

Welding Technology Engineer 78-79
   Metallurgy Engineer

ABOUT THIS BOOK

Probably no other phase of personnel guidance and job procurement techniques is quite as controversial as that which relates to job résumés. In the first place, some eminent authorities contend that résumés serve no purpose whatever; indeed, not infrequently, résumés hinder, rather than enhance, the applicant's chances for securing an interview. These authorities claim that a well-composed letter that singles out a few of the applicant's qualifications, enough to arouse the prospective employer's interest in meeting the applicant face to face, is far more effective than a formalized résumé that attempts to tell all.

Others, no less eminent in the field, call the résumé "the passport to a job interview." They have much evidence to back up that contention. All you have to do, they point out, is to glance through the classified section of any newspaper or recruitment literature and you'll see that, in most instances, a résumé is a standard prerequisite for a job interview—especially for better-paying positions.

Then, to add to the controversy, there are diametrically opposed points of view as to what should be included in a résumé. Some personnel specialists I have interviewed in the preparation of this book insist it's better to omit the Job Objective as a heading in a résumé. "Why limit your scope?" they say. Others point out it's advantageous to spell out the particular job you are looking for in the form of a Job Objective. How is your prospective employer to know the particular job you are aiming for if you apparently don't know, or at least won't state it in black and white. Some assert that it's necessary to include a reason for leaving to explain why you are looking for a job at the present time. Others contend that this is best left for the actual interview. And so it goes—each opinion is presented in the form of an inflexible dogma with a convenient rationale to go with it.

There are a number of helpful books on résumé-writing. Certainly this is not the first one. But this book is unique in this respect: the sample résumés that comprise the major portion of this book present a great variety of different styles of résumé construction, offering the reader the widest choice possible. If you leaf through these samples you will note that some résumés include a definite Job Objective, others do not. Some give priority to Education; some sublimate that aspect and emphasize Work Experience. A few give Reasons for Leaving. Most do not. The sample résumés shown vary considerably not only in content but in format as well. They did not all emerge from one résumé-making machine—same headings, same format, same length.

The résumés in this book have been carefully selected and edited, not to expound one man's (the author's) fixed idea of how a résumé should be written and presented, but to reflect a wide cross section of opinion arrived at through a national survey. The examples shown are modifications (both in content and form) of actual résumés, presented in photographically reduced proportion, to fit the page-size of this book. The layout—that is, how the typewritten copy is arranged on a page—comprises an important factor in the preparation of a résumé. The total effect of the format is achieved through the proper relationship of copy to surrounding space. To best see this relationship a gray tone was used on all résumé pages. This visual aid in showing résumés in facsimile form comprises an additional feature of the book and helps to differentiate it from similar publications.

In the final analysis, the personal résumé that you evolve should be distinctly your own—in format as well as in content. The intention of the author was to present a flexible guide to résumé construction, not a copy book. If this purpose is achieved, he will feel he has made a valuable contribution to the literature in the field.

In an early edition of Richard Nelson Bolles's *What Color Is Your Parachute?* in reference to this book he states, "If you believe in résumés (salvation by mail), this is the historic book in the field—a very thorough sampler of all kinds of résumés, together with helpful rationale."

Note: The practical value of this most recent edition of *Job Résumés* has been further expanded by presenting a greater number of résumés for women in managerial and executive positions. Included also is a select list of 100 questions which are most likely to come up during the course of the actual interview. Additional features include a Self-Appraisal Personality Scale, which anyone preparing for an interview may find helpful, and an updated bibliography of recommended reading relating to both résumé preparation and job interview techniques.

ILLUSTRATION
by
ED WALDMAN

According to the mailed-in (highly embellished) job résumé, the personnel director envisioned the applicant to look like the above.

In the actual face-to-face interview, the applicant shows his true-to-life appearance to be far different from expectations.

COMPILING DATA FOR YOUR JOB RÉSUMÉ

WHAT PURPOSE DOES A RÉSUMÉ SERVE?

For the best jobs today, a résumé is in most instances a prerequisite for a personal interview. Even if the particular job you are aiming for does not specifically call for a formal résumé, it's a good idea to get down on paper, briefly and succinctly, those aspects of your background that bear relevance to the job you seek. It's a good idea for many reasons. Here are some:

A résumé is helpful when you answer a want ad, either in writing or in person.

If the job applicant is to apply by mail, the employer generally expects a résumé, whether the ad specifically asks for it or not. There is a good reason for that. The position advertised—especially if it's an attractive one—may draw many responses. The average employer or personnel manager, or whoever it is that does the interviewing and hiring, has neither the time nor the patience to wade through stacks of letters replete with irrelevancies. Of prime importance is the applicant's specific qualifications. The employer is likely to favor the person who presents a fact sheet that is concise, to the point and in sequential order. That in effect describes what a résumé is—a presentation of pertinent facts that points up the applicant's fitness for the job on hand. For the employer, the résumé serves as a preliminary screening device in the selection of applicants to be interviewed. In the event the ad calls for the applicant to present himself in person, a well-organized résumé is still worth the trouble it takes to prepare it. A résumé serves as a crib sheet to jog your memory in the matter of dates, names and addresses of previous employers, schools attended, years of attendance, courses taken, and so on.

In case you are not hired on the spot (you can hardly expect that to happen on better jobs), you have a better chance to be remembered—and to be called back at a later time—if you leave a copy of your résumé with the interviewer. That is good advice even if you have gone through the routine of filling out the firm's employment application card. Often as not, the application does not provide sufficient space for supplementary information about yourself, which in your case may represent one of the highlights of your background. If you have a résumé on hand, your interviewer may either file it separately or attach it to your application. Either way you have improved your chances for getting the job.

A résumé serves as a functional "calling card" when you make the rounds of firms you would like to work for who have not placed an ad.

It takes a lot of stamina, persistence, and shoe leather to make "cold" contacts

9

—as salespeople call it. This course of action involves mapping out a route for making personal visits to a select number of firms you'd like to work for, in hopeful anticipation of getting an interview, with or without the formality of a previous appointment. Many sales are made that way; many good jobs are landed that way, too.

We are not here stressing the pros and cons of this course of action. What we are underscoring is this: a well-prepared résumé will be your best ally if you are venturesome enough to employ this direct approach to job procurement. If you do not get an interview or no present opening exists, you may leave a copy of your résumé for possible reference at a future time. In the event that you do get a personal interview, a résumé will help materially in the process of self-introduction. Modesty may inhibit you from talking about the honors you have won at school, citations you have received, sales records you have established. You'll be less reticent about making these known if you present the person who interviews you with a copy of your résumé which makes note of these highlights of your background, among other qualifications and credentials. The contents of the résumé invariably determines the direction the personal interview takes—and the impression you make.

You will make use of a résumé when you apply to an employment or personnel agency.

If you apply to an agency to help you locate a semiprofessional or professional position, such as chemical technician, sales manager, art director, engineer, programmer, or most of the better-paying jobs on a similar level, you can almost rest assured that you'll be asked to submit a résumé. This has become standard practice with a growing number of large agencies and indeed with most personnel departments of leading firms. The résumé is the fact sheet used to match staff needs of the employer with the qualifications of the job seeker.

Though a formal résumé is hardly ever a set requisite for the lower-paying jobs with minor responsibilities, most interviewers, consciously or not, are apt to be favorably disposed toward an applicant who has the foresight to come prepared with a résumé or well-organized fact sheet. The applicant benefits directly in another way by having on hand the needed facts to answer most of the important questions usually found on agency forms and application blanks.

A good résumé serves as the most effective mailing piece in a direct-mail job-search campaign.

Your sales pitch may include a personalized letter, a favorable clipping about yourself from a newspaper or trade publication, or even a reproduced sample of your work. It's the résumé, however, that often gets the most serious attention from prospective employers. Whether you organize your direct-mail campaign yourself, or have an agency handle it for you, the résumé is the one indispensable item in your entire job-search campaign via the mail.

A résumé makes it easier for those who know you to recommend you to potential employers.

It's surprising how many choice jobs are landed through word-of-mouth recommendations and "leads" by neighbors, relatives, friends and associates. Statistically, nearly one out of every four men and women gainfully employed today—on all levels from the mailroom clerk to the high-ranking executive—has found employment not merely on merit, but through personal recommendation. But you can hardly expect people to recommend you with any degree of confidence , or to steer you to a position compatible with your background and abilities, unless you make your qualifications known to them. Unquestionably, one of the most direct ways of achieving this is to supply your sponsors with a copy of your résumé. They can help you better if they know you better and have a résumé to refer to, or pass on to others.

A résumé serves another purpose not directly associated with job procurement. When you sit down to compile data for a résumé, you are forced, as it were, to take stock of your career up to the present. The résumé is a ledger which must show realistically, factually, almost impersonally, what you have accomplished so far, and which way you are heading. It's good to do this once in a while even if you are not immediately concerned with the task of looking for a job.

The primary purpose of this book, however, is to show you how to go about preparing a résumé with a specific vocational objective in mind. The information, advice or instruction—call it what you will—between the covers of this book will help you construct a successful job résumé, *custom-made to your personal requirements,* yet widely acceptable by employment agencies, personnel departments, executive recruiting firms, etc.

To help you in recalling and organizing pertinent data about two major aspects of your background, namely *Education* and *Work Experience,* you may find the forms on pages 25-26 helpful. Details as to these and various other aspects of your résumé will be discussed subsequently.

WHAT POINTS OF INFORMATION SHOULD A RÉSUMÉ INCLUDE?

Identification (who you are, where you can be reached)

Name: It's best to give your full name, spelling out the first, as well as the surname. Example: Robert Dunn, not R. Dunn. The use of an initial forces the employer to guess what the initial stands for and whether the applicant is male or female. The applicant's gender may be gleaned from the general context of the résumé, but why annoy the employer with guessing games?

Address: Give complete address with a minimum of abbreviations. When used for states, the post office recommends its official two-letter designations. And always include your ZIP CODE.

Phone number: You may, if you wish, include two phone numbers—your home phone and your business phone, if you are currently employed. Hint: Before you give out your business number for personal reasons, clear it with your boss, especially if you hopefully expect a barrage of incoming calls from prospective employers. Your sudden popularity may prove a source of embarrassment to you and may even be the cause of losing your present job before you've had time to switch.

Objective

Experts in the field of personnel and employment differ strongly as to whether a definite Job Objective should be stated in a résumé. Some say a Job Objective (Position Desired, Employment Goal, or similar heading) seriously limits the scope of employment. "Why specify a position either by a title or phrase that may not exactly correspond to an existing vacancy?" they ask. "If you don't pin yourself down to a specific job title, you leave the door open to be considered for one or more alternate positions—perhaps as good if not better than the one you had in mind." Others contend that very few employers will want to take the trouble to analyze your résumé in the hope of guessing what position you are looking for. State the job you want and define it as clearly and concisely as possible.

Use your own best judgment as to which reasoning to follow. Should you be versatile enough to qualify with equal confidence in two or more fields not necessarily related, the best advice is: prepare a distinct and separate résumé, each with its own job objective, custom-made to accent those qualifications which match the job you seek.

Personnel agencies catering to top-level positions often omit the heading *Objective* on résumés designated for important clients.

If, for whatever reason that seems logical to you, you decide to include a Job Objective in your résumé, it is sometimes helpful to state it in the form of a thumbnail synopsis. Example: "Young man, college graduate, with two years of practical experience in publishing, doing paste-ups and mechanicals, seeks position with advertising agency to do layout and design. Special interest in packaging." This statement, which reads like a Situation Wanted ad, accomplishes several things: it helps to introduce the applicant; it focuses attention on salient qualifications that are developed in depth in the body of the résumé; it clearly indicates a vocational objective.

Education

Schools you have attended: It is cus-

tomary to list these in *reverse* chronological order; i.e., the last school attended listed first, and so on down the line. In each case, include name and location of school, dates of attendance, diploma or degree conferred.

If you have contributed appreciably to financing your education, it would not be amiss to make reference to this, as evidence of enterprise, initiative and self-determination to pay your own way. "Financed major portion of school expenses through personal earnings and savings" adds a positive note to the résumé of any young person about to enter the workaday world. If your college education was financed by winning a scholarship, this fact deserves mention under the general heading of Education.

Major courses and grades: You may make reference to, or actually list, major courses. Do so only if they bear a definite and important relationship to your present professional interests, or the job you seek. If your grades were exceptionally high, list them. If not, don't advertise the fact. In general, give more space to your school history if you are a recent graduate with little or no work experience. If you are a mature job seeker with a number of degrees to your credit or have completed your schooling a long time ago, it would serve very little purpose to allude to more than the last two or three schools attended. Don't give space to your elementary or junior high school record. Nobody cares. It's what you have done since that counts.

In professional fields, such as medicine, engineering, or chemistry, it is often helpful to list technical courses taken, to pinpoint the area of specialization.

Extracurricular activities: This, as a subheading under Education, may call attention to some of the extracurricular activities in which you participated, or excelled. Example: vice-president of the senior class, member of the publications committee, director of the art club, library aide. Did you excel in sports? This can be a point in your favor, as an indication of physical agility, team spirit, leadership potential.

If you have had an extensive extracurricular record, you can be selective, singling out those activities that relate to your professional goal and have a direct bearing on the job you are presently seeking. Naturally, the more mature you are and the more practical work experience you have, the less space you will devote to school-oriented activities.

Work Experience

This section includes the following information: name and location of each firm you worked for, dates of employment, what your responsibilities entailed and, where possible, how well you carried out these responsibilities. It is customary to list the work-experience record in reverse chronological order, starting with the current employer and going back.

In compiling such information and allocating space to this phase of your résumé, bear this in mind: your prospective employer wants to know your entire employment history, but he or she is particularly interested in your most recent job—one which presumably represents your highest level of achievement. Give this the most space.

Firms you worked for: List each firm, giving general location—city and state are sufficient. Don't waste space on street and zone number. The small companies you worked for may require identification as to the nature of their products and services, and perhaps a word or two to in-

dicate position in the field. If you have worked for General Motors, IBM, or an organization of similar stature, you need not sing its praises. You may, however, want to specify the branch or division you worked for.

Dates of employment: Indicate the years in which you began and left each firm; for short duration jobs, include the months. Don't leave any "holes" in the chronology of employment. Any unexplained gap will easily be spotted as the employer scans the dates. A break in the continuity may be open to suspicion or, at least, to question.

Title and Responsibilities: For each job listed, indicate responsibilities as well as title. A title or payroll position such as Department Supervisor, Managing Editor, or Art Director, while suggesting in a general way the function of the position, does not reveal the nature and extent of the responsibilities. The position of department supervisor, for example, may involve supervisory responsibilities for two or three persons, or for a work force of 150.

Describe briefly the major and related responsibilities for each job shown. In some cases it is desirable also to list skills and familiarity with specific equipment, processes and techniques.

Whenever possible give evidence of how well you carried out your responsibilities. Just to state you were eminently successful in all you have undertaken is at best a generality. What lends substance to claims are statistics. A sales manager's statement that he was "instrumental in increasing sales" is made more meaningful if it is backed up with figures showing percentage increase in volume of business or company profits, directly attributable to his efforts. It helps considerably to give a sampling of activities which brought about the results shown—developing new markets, setting up a sales-incentive program, liaison with production or research to improve quality of product while decreasing the production and distribution costs, and so on. If you have developed a new idea or system, that's fine; but the more important thing is how it was beneficial to the company. Was it a success? Back up your claims!

If your work experience is diversified or has extended over a long span of years involving frequent job changes, it is sometimes advisable to categorize your employment record *functionally* rather than chronologically. A functional pattern features a range of abilities or areas of experience rather than a year-by-year summary of uninterrupted employment. In a functional résumé, names of employers and specific dates are of secondary importance and may in some instances be omitted in part, or entirely.

In organizing your résumé on a functional basis, list each area of experience under a separate heading. Include under each, your function, responsibilities, and proven accomplishments. For an example of a functional résumé, see pages 42-43.

Generally speaking, the more prevalent type of résumé is one based on a chronological arrangement. Most of the résumés shown in this book are of this type.

Personal Data

This can be brief, expanded or omitted entirely, depending upon the type of job you are looking for and the amount of space available on the résumé. For instance, if you are aiming for a position as athletic coach, detailed physical specifications are relatively more significant than they would be for a position as re-

searcher or accountant.

The heading *Personal Data* on the résumé may or may not include date of birth, height, weight, marital status, number of dependents, condition of health, etc. Color of eyes or hair is hardly ever relevant. What if your eyes are azure blue? Will that make you a better auditor? There are situations, however, when selected details as to physical attributes may bear vocational relevance. An applicant endowed with a beautiful head of hair aiming for a job in the promotion department of a hair lotion manufacturer might conceivably improve his or her chances for landing the job by alluding to this personal characteristic in the résumé.

The question of age may possibly be of some concern to job seekers past forty. If it bothers you, don't call attention to your age by noting specific date of birth. For some time now it has been considered discriminatory labor practice for employers to use age as a determining factor in the hiring of personnel and *date of birth* no longer has a place on application blanks of equal opportunity employers.

Though height and weight may appear on a résumé, weight is perhaps a more significant item. Obesity may suggest glandular malfunction, lack of physical agility and in some cases ungainly appearance. If you are of normal weight for your age and height, you may state it. If not, omit this item in the hope that during the interview your other fine personal and professional qualifications will more than make up for this physical shortcoming and that it in no way interferes with the performance of your duties. Use your best judgment here, as you would in the case of a physical disability. Space permitting, you may want to state the condition of your health. If it's excellent, say so. In some instances, you may want to include the date of your last medical checkup.

Your marital status has some significant connotations. As far as the résumé goes, you are either single, married, or widowed. If you are divorced, you are, for all practical purposes, single. There may be some residual prejudice lingering in the mind of your potential employer in hiring a person whose marriage didn't work out, ending in divorce, annulment, or separation. There may even be the lurking, though unfounded, suspicion of a security risk in hiring someone with present or past domestic complications.

For some positions, employers look favorably upon an applicant who is married and has a family. Such a person seems to represent greater stability, one less likely to be a job hopper. If you have children, you may say how many, but need not go into particulars about their names and ages. For positions involving considerable travel, the single person with no dependents may have the advantage.

Under the *Personal Data* heading you may wish to state whether you own or rent the home you live in, and if you own a car. If you are willing to relocate and/or travel, there is an advantage in pointing that out in your résumé.

Mention your hobbies if they bear a relation to the position you are seeking. For example, if you apply for a position as security guard in a bank or similar institution, mention of active interest in athletics is a point in your favor. If it's a journalist job you're after, photography as a hobby and avocation is worthy of mention, since photography and journalism—especially reportorial journalism—quite often go hand in hand.

Military History

If you have had a distinguished career in the armed services, it is important to give it space in the job résumé only if the job you are seeking bears some relationship to that experience. For example, if you served in the quartermaster division where you were responsible for purchases and inventory of military supplies, this information certainly would reflect in your favor as an applicant for a position where purchasing and inventory control constitute some of the main functions of the job.

Use discretion in the allotment of space on the job résumé for service in the armed forces. Ask yourself, "Will this information help me get the job I want?"

Affiliations

This heading may include membership in professional organizations, learned societies, and significant social and civic groups. For most jobs, it's wise to omit religious and strongly political affiliations since they may be contrary to the sentiments and commitments of your potential employer. An active and wide acquaintanceship is a particular asset for people in sales, real estate and insurance. An applicant with a large circle of acquaintances presumably has a broader field of operation. "Every friend is a potential customer."

References

Seasoned employers do not regard references on a résumé too seriously—at least, not until they are ready to hire you. The real interest in checking your character reference, as well as other credentials, will come after you have made a good impression in a personal interview. Under the heading of *References* it is sufficient to indicate that they are available and can be submitted upon request.

FORMAT AND PHYSICAL APPEARANCE OF JOB RÉSUMÉS

Length of résumé

Limit your résumé to one or two pages. If it is at all possible condense the informaton to fit on one page without crowding. This advice is corroborated by most employment agents and personnel managers who receive hundreds of unsolicited résumés each week. Some go as far as to say, in no uncertain terms, that they won't read a résumé over one page in length; that their dormant files are full of three- and four-page dissertations representing the hopeful career aspirations of ingenuous applicants. A résumé, whether it be unsolicited or in response to a specific job vacancy, should be short in words, but not in facts.

There are singular exceptions to this call for brevity. A case in point is a résumé outlining the special qualifications and heavy professional background of top-level executives in the $85,000-and-up salary bracket. Often such résumés are brochure-length presentations prepared by executive-search specialists as part of a "packaged" job-search campaign. Even in such instances, many experts feel that a well-organized one- or two-page résumé can be more effective in securing the attention of prospective employers than an overly long buildup of alleged qualifications.

Kind and size of paper

Don't deviate from the standard 8-½" x 11" size just to be different. A variation in size (either larger or smaller) can prove to be more annoying than distinctive. An odd size requires special handling since most filing systems are made for 8-½" x 11" paper. Unless you are in the creative arts or in promotion and want the résumé to serve as a sample of your professional talents, don't break step with tradition. Let the "pros" take the risk.

Use the best quality paper you can get, whether it be white or softly tinted. The difference in cost between a good quality and poor quality paper is negligible compared to what is at stake. "Good paper makes a good impression" is a slogan in the paper industry. It's true in more ways than one. A fine quality paper takes typing and printing better, and enhances the total effect of the résumé.

Typing: methods of reproducing duplicate copies

Since an extensive job search campaign may call for hundreds of duplicate résumés, it is essential that the master copy be literally and figuratively "letter perfect." Bear in mind that the reproduction can only be as good as the original. Unless you consider yourself an excellent typist, it's wisest to get your résumé typed professionally. A résumé showing uneven pressure, irregular alignment of characters, erasures and/or other evidence of human or mechanical struggle can seriously hurt your chances to be granted a personal interview. Today, professional typists have at their command state-of-the-art word processors and electronic and laser typewriters which permit a wide variation in type characters as well as size and weight of type. What is more, corrections and revisions are easily made without undue effort.

There are a number of ways to get multiple copies, but definitely rule out duplicates produced by carbon sheets. It is most unflattering to any prospective employer to be on the receiving end of a résumé reproduced in this manner. The wiser course of action is to make duplicates by the Xerox or similar photocopying processes. Technically, modern photocopying processes are capable of producing facsimiles that are hardly distinguishable from the master copy. Cost of reproduction of individual copies is negligible compared to the results achieved–the range being anywhere from 10 to 20 cents per copy, and considerably less in larger quantities. The greater the number of copies, the smaller the unit price. Also, the inherent advantages of photocopying methods is that the original can be reproduced same size, larger or smaller as required.

Résumés set in traditional printer's type and reproduced by the photo-offset method cost more but yield the highest quality reproduction. This method is generally reserved for large distribution.

Arrangement and page layout

You don't have to be an artist to arrange the wording in your résumé to be typographically effective. A résumé is essentially an outline. Keep it that way— simple, consistent and uncluttered.

A well-arranged résumé is easy to look at; it is easy to read. To achieve this, organize your wording into compact paragraphs or thought groups under main and secondary headings. To accent salient points of information, such as duties, job titles, names of schools and firms, you may want to use underscoring or capitalization. This also helps to add variety and typographic interest to a page of copy. Leave lots of white space. There is no fixed pattern or standard layout. Experiment, if you like, to introduce a note of individuality, but keep this within bounds.

We advised previously, *leave lots of white space*. That's easier said than done. The chances are good that your résumé will require three, four, or more complete revisions, both in wording and in arrange-

ment, before you manage to fit all the information on one or two pages, without evidence of overcrowding. It's been said, "The white space on the paper makes the printed space easy to read." Even professional résumé writers revise copy and layout several times before they arrive at a good presentation—one that is chock-full of pertinent information, yet looks uncluttered and is easy to read. Compare the two résumés on pages 34 and 35 to see how appearance and readability are improved not only because of change in wording, but also because of the typographic arrangement.

THE LANGUAGE OF JOB RÉSUMÉS

Résumés are written in a language not unlike that used in classified ads or auditors' reports. The style is factual, concise and space-conserving. A résumé briefly and almost impersonally states who you are, what your qualifications are, and the kind of service you can render to an employer.

A résumé is a statement of facts, not opinions, generalizations or personal convictions, no matter how noble. "It has always been my fervent hope . . . ," and other such strong personal or editorial comments have no place in a résumé.

Use active verbs, such as *organized, increased, administered, designed, directed,* and *initiated.* To make for easier reading, use short, simple words: *try* for *endeavor; varied* for *multifarious; get* for *obtain;* and so forth.

In a résumé it is customary to limit the use of first person singular (I, me, my, mine) not merely to conserve space, but also to be freer to mention accomplishments without giving the impression of boasting. For transmittal letters, letters of application and similar correspondence, in which a more personal approach is appropriate, there need not be any arbitrary restrictions in the use of personal pronouns.

General Phraseology

Here are some examples of expressions and phrases applicable to certain aspects of the résumé. You may find these helpful both in the choice of words as well as in content.

JOB OBJECTIVE

- Opportunity to utilize technical and supervisory experience in the field of____.
- Offer ____ years of practical experience in _____, qualifying for a position as _____.
- A _____ position utilizing interest and training in the _____ industry.
- _____ trainee leading to account executive position with progressive organization.
- Major interest in a position in _____ with opportunity for further specialization later.
- To be affiliated with a _____ company as _____ where responsibility may lead to top management level.

Here in full is a somewhat different and more individual approach.

- A "Gal Friday" who operates equally well every day of the week seeks challenging position in busy advertising office.

EDUCATIONAL BACKGROUND

- Graduated in upper ____ percent of class.
- Financed expenses with ____-year scholarship.
- _____ percent expenses financed by personal earnings and past savings.

- On Dean's List during ____ years of college.
- Earned special commendation for highest achievement in _____.

(If you don't have any degrees or diplomas to indicate extensive formal education, you may wish to choose from the following examples.)

- Have taken courses in _____ at _____ as part of self-improvement program.
- Have successfully completed company-sponsored training program in _____.
- Passed ____-year, college-level test while in service.
- Extensive home-study course in ____.
- Completed _____ years technical training courses at _____.
- Following high school graduation, have taken variety of courses whenever time and employment permitted. These include: _____, _____, _____, _____.
- As a plan for continued study in the field of _____, have completed the following courses: _____, _____, _____.

WORK EXPERIENCE (showing evidence of growth or special achievement.)

- Promoted to _____ position with enlarged responsibilities and ____ percent increase in salary.
- Within ____ years of employment with the company, was promoted to the following positions: _____, _____, each with a substantial increase in salary.
- As supervisor of the _____ department, initiated a new system of _____, which reduced yearly operating costs by _____ percent and increased profits by over $__.
- Started as _____ with a staff of ____.

Within ____ years was promoted to position of _____ with a staff of ____, and salary increase of ____.

- In my capacity as _____, had direct supervision of ____ employees.
- Have working knowledge of operation and maintenance of the following equipment: _____, _____, _____, _____.
- Have the following secretarial skills: typing: ____ words per minute; stenography: ____ words per minute. In addition, can operate the following office machines: _____, _____, _____, _____.
- Yearly income increased by $ ____ during period of employment.
- Started as _____, promoted to position of _____ within a period of ____ years.

Here is a sample of a statement, in full:

As Administrative Assistant to the Vice-President, duties ranged from writing sales-promotion letters to creating, scheduling and administrating sales-incentive programs and contests. When the company decided to enter the supermarket field, I was assigned to survey this field and upon my recommendations, our sales force was increased from a staff of 16 to 32 and its entire method of distribution was altered. Today, all major supermarkets and chain stores throughout the country have the full line of our products on display. Company profits have risen more than 30 percent each consecutive year.

REASONS FOR LEAVING

- To accept better position offering greater opportunities.
- To be discussed at interview.
- Left to complete college education.
- Merger of departments.
- Work was seasonal. Wished to secure steady employment.
- Firm relocated to different part of country.
- Little opportunity for further advancement.
- Desire to expand experience beyond the scope of present position.
- Left on amicable terms. Have letter of reference and commendation.
- Was offered and accepted position which promised greater scope.

REFERENCES

- On request. Please do not contact present employer before interview.
- Portfolio of work available for review.
- References on hand, and available.
- A personal interview will provide the opportunity to review my portfolio and to explore my qualifications.
- Copies of transcript of record and letters of recommendation available.
- Inquiries as to personal qualities and work record may be addressed to:

PERSONAL INFORMATION

- Own home; late model car.
- Rent apartment; free to travel as required.
- Served in Peace Corps from _____ to _____.
- Finances in good order. No debt encumbrances.
- Speak, read and write the following languages: _____, _____.
- Available for full- or part-time work.
- Currently employed. Available upon ____ days' notice.
- Security Clearance; Top Secret.
- Active in local and national civic organizations as time permits.
- Within limitations of time, have been active in community and civic projects such as _____, _____, _____.

- Member of the following professional associations: _____, _____, _____.
- Excellent health, last medical checkup _____.
- Varied outside interests include _____, _____, _____.
- Well groomed, good personal appearance, friendly disposition.
- Willing to relocate.
- Job-related hobbies: _____, _____, _____.

SALARY

- Currently earning $ _____ per year.
- Negotiable.
- Commensurate with opportunity offered.
- Salary range: $ _____ to $ _____.
- Salary to be discussed during interview.
- Opportunity to learn, rather than starting salary, is of major importance.
- Salary on last job: $ _____.

MILITARY SERVICE

- Veteran, honorable discharge. Served from _____ to _____.
- Saw service in _____, _____.
- Received special training in _____.
- Separated from military service with rank of _____.
- Honorary military citations include _____, _____, _____.

LETTERS

Cover or Transmittal Letter

No résumé should be placed in an envelope and mailed off without a cover letter. If the résumé is in response to a specific job vacancy the cover letter should refer to the vacancy and call attention to the résumé, which shows how well your total qualifications match the requirements of the job. Or else the letter may single out one aspect of your general qualifications that you feel will be of special interest to your prospective employer—an aspect developed in greater detail in the résumé. Whenever feasible, personalize your correspondence by addressing the letter, as well as the envelope, to a particular individual, using his or her official title. You can check the spelling of the name and verify the title by phoning for this information. In the event you do not know the identity of the advertiser (as would be the case in answering a blind ad with a box number) begin your letter with either Personnel Manager, Manager of Personnel Department, or some such salutation—never with "To whom it may concern."

A cover letter should be brief and businesslike, and yet it should introduce a personal touch to distinguish it from routine correpondence. It should introduce the applicant and arouse the interest of the employer sufficiently so that the applicant's résumé will be given due consideration, thus paving the way for an invitation for a personal interview.

For a sampling of cover letters, see pages 28, 29, and 30.

The "Broadcast" Letter

This type of direct-mail promotion, commonly referred to as a "broadcast" letter, has many exponents among personnel counselors who claim it to be an excellent way—some say that it is by far the best way—when soliciting job interviews through the mail.

The broadcast letter is mailed without a résumé. It is a short one-page synopsis highlighting the applicant's qualifications, equated purely on proven achievements. These are expressed in simple terse sentences, wherever possible quoting facts, figures and percentages. The essential function of this type of correspondence is to arouse an interest in the applicant and cause the employer to want to know more through a personal interview. Whereas a formal résumé generally goes into details about the varied aspects of the applicant's total background, education, experience, personal data and so on, the broadcast letter does not. In a sense, the broadcast letter is a preliminary to a résumé; it is not a substitute for one. A formal résumé will still be needed later, either during the actual interview, or as a follow-up.

For a sample broadcast letter, see page 27.

QUESTIONS AND ANSWERS RELATING TO RÉSUMÉ PREPARATION

As a recent graduate, how can I list work experience when I haven't had any?

You may have had work experience without realizing it; you may have held a part-time or summer job, been in "business for yourself" running a paper route, cared for lawns in your neighborhood, or engaged in other self-employment chores. In addition, you may have acquired practical work skills in your extracurricular activities at school—selling advertising space for the school publications, operating a copying machine, typing term papers, or tutoring with or without payment. Tabulate your experience and work skills, list them and then select those that relate to the job you want. Give yourself credit for these work experiences in or out of school, though you may not have held down a regular nine-to-five job.

Again and again we are told that résumés should be brief—no more than one or two pages in length. Why this emphasis on brevity?

This call for brevity requires some qualification. In preparing a résumé for unsolicited distribution, it is no doubt best to get all your facts down on one page. The situation is somewhat different if you are preparing a résumé in answer to an advertised job vacancy and you have some basis for assuming that the employer is as anxious to find a qualified worker as you are to find a potential employer. As an occasional advertiser the employer is not inundated with résumés, as are personnel directors of major corporations, and is therefore more apt to read your résumé with sustained interest, even if it is extensive—especially if you are a person with unique skills. Generally speaking, however, the more concise the résumé, the better.

Why is it so few job résumés include photographs of applicants?

For one thing, it may be construed as discriminatory for employers or employment agencies to require job applicants to submit photographs. Then too, except in unusual cases, as for example in show business, where physical appearance is often of professional importance, photographs serve very little purpose. In fact, they are potentially harmful. Your prospective employer may not like the way you part your hair (he may have none to part) or may think your ears are too large or your lips too thin. He may have a natural antipathy, which even he does not recognize, for the type of person your photograph represents you to be. Photography as an art is highly advanced, but the average snapshot type of photo is often unflattering and does little to enhance the value of your résumé.

Is there a prescribed sequence for the various headings in a résumé?

No. The sequence is optional and will depend largely upon the qualifications you feature and the position you seek. If you are a recent graduate with only your good scholastic record to speak for you, you may want to give priority to your academic background by giving it top billing. The résumé of a mature sales manager, on the other hand, with many years of successful work experience will list the employment record first.

I have held five different jobs with as many companies in less than four years. Should my résumé indicate "reason for leaving" in each case?

No. It isn't necessary, or advisable, to state the reason for leaving each job, especially if you were dismissed. You can explain the circumstances verbally if the subject comes up during the course of the interview. At no time, however, either in writing or in person, should you indulge in recrimination about former employers.

A lengthy explanation about why you left each job not only takes up valuable space in a résumé, but tends to dramatize the number of jobs you've held and may identify you either as a chronic job hopper or an incompetent, malcontent employee.

A brief statement such as "left to widen scope of opportunities" or "accepted position with more responsibilities and higher salary" is quite appropriate. But don't overdo even that, if it creates an obvious pattern.

How can I make my résumé different from those customarily received by agencies and employers?

Perhaps the most effective way to accomplish this is to see to it that your résumé is neat, well organized, and free from typographic or grammatical discrepancies. If you are artistically inclined or can get professional assistance, then including an appropriate graphic symbol or personal logo relating to the position you seek could add visual impact. On occasion, signing your name at the bottom of the résumé with pen or colored felt marker helps to personalize the résumé.

As to the wording of the résumé, avoid tacky gimmicks and hyperbole. Example: Enclosing an aspirin tablet with a phrase such as "Mr. Employer, do you have an insurmountable sales promotion problem? Here's your remedy—*me!*" Another such example: Singeing the edges of the résumé and featuring a headline, "This is the hottest news in the industry," accompanied with a brief text that shows the revolutionary nature of an idea the writer of the résumé has developed. Generally speaking, it's best to stay within the bounds of propriety.

For a rather safe departure from the average presentation, you may want to experiment using a slightly off-white or tinted paper. The printed matter for legibility's sake should be black, regardless of the color of the paper.

Does the general appearance of a résumé make much difference as long as the facts are there?

It always makes a difference, but to a varying degree, depending upon the nature of the job you are looking for and how much the prospective employer needs your services. If you apply for a job as a proofreader or secretary and your résumé has a sprinkling of errors in spelling and grammar, the "facts" outlined in your résumé attesting to your proficiency are automatically discredited. In this and similar instances, your résumé is in effect a sample of your work. On the other hand, if your talents, services or skills are so exclusive that you have a minimum of competition in your field—and a job opening must be filled quickly—it will be the *contents*, rather than the appearance of your résumé which is of prime importance. Normally, the appearance of the résumé makes a first impression on the employer—even before getting down to the facts.

Be sure that your résumé is not only factually impressive but visually impressive as well.

Should the matter of salary be included in a job résumé?

Salary is an optional item on a résumé. However, there are strategic reasons for its usual omission. If you stipulate too high a salary, you may price yourself out of the picture; if too low, you undersell yourself. If you wish, you may resort to the expediency of stating that salary is negotiable, giving a general salary range, or of mentioning your most recent salary.

In most instances, the salary question is best deferred to the time of the interview. At that time you can size up the situation more realistically in terms of the firm's prevailing salary scale and the extent of your work responsibilities.

In the case of a physical disability, is it considered "withholding information" if you do not refer to it on the résumé?

The phrase "withholding information" seems to have legal connotations. You are not guilty of breaking a legal or even mor-

al code if you omit mentioning a physical disability that may prejudice your chances for an interview. If, however, the nature of your disability is a serious one, and may cause you embarrassment and loss of confidence if it comes as a total surprise to your interviewer, then it's best to make mention of the disability with some factual assurance that it has not impeded you in the performance of duties in the past.

Is it necessary to get the approval of anyone you intend to list as a reference, even though you feel quite certain that you will be highly recommended?

Yes, by all means. Your reference will be able to anticipate an inquiry about you and be mentally prepared with a statement of considered opinions and facts. It's especially important, also, to let that person know how many such inquiries to expect. For instance, if Mr. John Smith is your reference on a résumé distributed to hundreds of prospective employers, he may be justifiably annoyed at the number of inquiries that reach him by phone or mail. Unless he is apprised of the extent of your intended distribution, he may show his annoyance at the intrusion either by ignoring all inquiries or perhaps giving an unfavorable report. Good advice is therefore to obtain permission of the people you list as references and to inform them of the nature of the position you are looking for and the number of inquiries they may expect. It's also a good idea to give them copies of your résumé. For all you know, they may turn out to be good sources of job leads, now or in the future.

What is the consensus regarding résumés written by hand?

Unless you are particularly and justifiably proud of your handwriting, and the nature of the job bears some relation to the quality of your script, current business practice calls for a typewritten résumé.

It may be a point of interest for you to know that a number of large corporations place great importance on handwriting as a revealing factor in personality analysis of job applicants. To the discerning eye of expert graphologists employed by these corporations, a person's handwriting may reveal not merely obvious characteristics related to emotional stability, but specific aptitudes, leadership qualities, general work habits—even physical appearance.

Since most employers have neither the inclination, time nor ability to analyze your handwriting, it's preferable, except in singular instances, to show the best of your personal qualities and other qualifications in type, not script.

Should my résumé omit the heading of Education in the absence of degrees or diplomas? Though I have taken a variety of courses throughout the years, my formal education has been limited.

It would be a serious omission to entirely bypass your educational background simply because you have no diplomas or degrees. Your résumé should make mention of specific training programs you have completed, schools you have attended, courses you have taken and other evidence of self-improvement. An effort in this direction often makes a favorable impression on a prospective employer. Make the most of it!

In this as well as other aspects of your job résumé, select the facts that put you in your best light. Accentuate the positive.

Is it necessary to mention hobbies in a résumé?

Only if space permits and if they relate to the field of vocational interest. If you apply for a position as a piano tuner, it would be pointless to mention the fact that you are an expert scuba diver. If photography is your hobby and you are in the field of journalism, printing, or selling photography supplies, obviously your hobby strengthens and supplements your vocational interest. If you end up with extra space on the résumé, you may mention your hobbies, guided by the above advice.

Is there any advantage in getting professional help in preparing a résumé?

If by professional help you mean slight revision in the basic wording, and preparing a master copy for printing, the answer is yes. Most résumé printers, for a reasonable fee, will help you to that extent. But for the most part it shouldn't prove necessary to engage the services of professional résumé preparers. Professionally prepared résumés may not only be costly, but often tend to smack of super-professionalism which could well be out of keeping with the nature of the position applied for and the background of the job applicant.

The information as well as the wide variety of sample résumés shown in this book should serve as adequate guidelines for you to prepare your own résumé.

SUMMARY OF WORK EXPERIENCE

Date of employment: from _____ to _____

Name and address of company: _____

_____

Company's products or services consist of: _____

_____

Name and title of immediate supervisor: _____

My title or position with the company: _____

My primary responsibilities included: _____

_____

_____

My secondary responsibilities included: _____

_____

_____

Specific examples showing how effectively I fulfilled my responsibilities:

_____

_____

List of skills, processes, and techniques relating to responsibilities:

_____

_____

Name and title of person most likely to give me a good reference:

_____

Salary: when I began _____ when I left _____

Reason for leaving: _____

SUMMARY OF EDUCATIONAL BACKGROUND

Years of attendance: from _____ to _____

Name and location of school: _____
_____

Diploma or degree earned: _____

Major courses of study: _____
_____
_____
_____

Related courses of study: _____
_____
_____
_____

Position or standing in class: _____

Awards, citations, scholarships: _____
_____
_____

Extracurricular activities: _____
_____
_____

Name and title of persons most likely to give me good references:
_____
_____
_____

SUGGESTED FORM FOR COMPILING EDUCATION DATA

JOHN DOE   100 CONVENT ROAD, SYOSSET, NY 11791   (516) 100-0000

January 14, 1990

Mr. John Jones, President
Snyder Industries, Inc.
733 Third Avenue
New York, NY 10017

Dear Mr. Jones:

In my four years as General Sales Manager of a leading
construction distributor in upstate New York, I directed the
sales and leasing policies of the company line of
products--power equipment for heavy construction industries.

During that time:

- Annual billings in outright sales and term rentals
  increased from $7.5 million to $11.75 million.

- Profits rose five-fold, from $180,000 in 1985 to
  $940,000 for the fiscal year ending May, 1989.

- Number of accounts have increased more than 400%.

The success I've had here and elsewhere in 12 years of
selling is not a coincidence, or attributable to luck or
magic. My special education in Business Administration
(Harvard grad.) has helped some; more important than that is
a natural ability to analyze a production-selling situation,
and come up with an innovative program that leaves
competition way behind.

What I have done for others, I am confident I can do for
you.

I would be glad to make myself available for a personal
interview where we can discuss how I can serve your company.

Sincerely yours,

John Doe

John Doe

EXAMPLE OF AN EFFECTIVE BROADCAST LETTER   27

100 Northern Boulevard
New York, NY 10468
January 8, 1990

Mr. John Jones, President
Jones, Smith and Associates
1620 Broadway
New York, NY 10036

Dear Mr. Jones:

Your display ad in last Sunday's Times for an Art Director in Cosmetic Package Design is of special interest to me because it calls for qualifications which completely correspond to my background and job objective.

You will note from my résumé (herewith enclosed) that in addition to an excellent professional background in general advertising with emphasis on cosmetics, I have had particular success in package design, having twice this year been awarded citations by the Package Council for outstanding innovations in cosmetic merchandising.

It is time for me to move on to a company such as yours, which I consider to be one of the most progressive young packaging design agencies in the field. I am young too, and at 27 have had five years of hardcore experience--and am ready for new challenges which I know will await me as art director with your firm.

May I ask you to read the résumé and permit me to phone your secretary next week for an appointment? I will have my portfolio with me and I look forward to meeting with you.

Sincerely yours,

Jane Doe

Jane Doe

Telephone:
100-0000

100 North Carlton Avenue
Camden, NJ 09170
January 5, 1990

Mr. John Jones, Personnel Manager
S & W Food Processing Company, Inc.
1510 East Main Street
Camden, NJ 09170

Dear Mr. Jones:

In response to your ad in the January 4 issue of the Camden Inquirer, I am taking the liberty of forwarding a personal résumé touching upon certain aspects of my technical background which should prove to be of special interest to you at this time. As you will note, my entire training and work experience in food processing run parallel to the demands of this position.

I am currently employed as Chemical Engineer with the Royal Food Company, 1420 Broad Street, Camden, NJ. For reference, you may contact my superior, Mr. Thomas Benson, whom I have apprised of my intention to leave under the most amicable circumstances.

I will be glad to make myself available for an interview at any time suited to your convenience.

Sincerely yours,

John Doe

John Doe

Telephone:
100-0000

CLIPPING OF AD

100 Blue Island Avenue
Chicago, Illinois 60607
January 10, 1990

Ms. Jane Jones, Personnel Manager
Barkeley Photos, Inc.
120 East Wacker Drive
Chicago, Illinois 60601

Dear Ms. Jones:

As a recent graduate, I understandably have not as yet had much opportunity to gain solid work experience other than part-time and summer employment listed on the résumé, herewith enclosed. Incidentally, these after-school jobs not only furthered my interest and practical experience in photography, but helped materially in financing my college tuition.

Right through college, photography has been my professional goal (as some of the courses listed will show), with the hope some day to be affiliated with a progressive photo research laboratory such as yours. That day has now come.

I believe that my educational and technical background as well as my experience (limited though it may be) can be utilized by your firm to advantage, and I look forward to an interview when I may have the opportunity to discuss with you employment possibilities. I have a portfolio of samples and the best of references.

I will take the liberty of phoning you early next week for an appointment.

Sincerely yours,

John Doe

John Doe

Home telephone:
100-0000

PORTFOLIO OF SAMPLE RÈSUMÈS

RÉSUMÉ FORMATS AND LAYOUTS

GOOD

Symmetric (formal balance) arrangement, appropriate for functional-type résumé.

GOOD

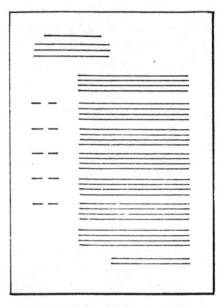

Asymmetric (informal balance) arrangement, appropriate for chronological-type résumé.

FAULTY

Too much copy and inadequate margins, resulting in a crowded effect.

FAULTY

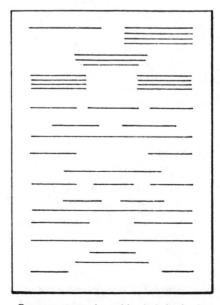

Copy too scattered, resulting in lack of unity and cohesion.

JOB OBJECTIVE

State type of job you would like with the company. For example: A beginning job in _____ leading to a position as _____ _____.

EDUCATION

Name of schools and years attended, degrees you hold, major subject field, special courses, awards and citations. (Space permitting, list courses which relate to the job you are seeking.)

EXTRACURRICULAR ACTIVITIES OR OUTSIDE INTERESTS

Select and list those school and club activities, hobbies or other outside interests which have a direct or tangential bearing on your job objective.

EXPERIENCE

List all part-time, summer or volunteer jobs you have held. Show how this work experience (limited though it may be) has a valuable application to your present job objective and future vocational goal.

Include useable work skills you have acquired, both in and out of school: typing, operating business machines, fluency in foreign languages, and so forth.

PERSONAL DATA

Date of birth:_____   Health:_____
Height:_____   Marital status: _____
Weight:_____   Language skills:_____

REFERENCES

(This is an optional heading.) You may want to list names and addresses of several people who know you well enough to recommend you. In most instances, it is sufficient to say, "References Available."

                              BILL BAXTER
                           100 West 181 Street
                           New York, NY 10038
                            (212) 100-0000

OBJECTIVE: Part time (after school hours and/or weekends),
                to work as copy boy or in similar capacity in
                newspaper office, hoping eventually to enter
                professional field in reportorial journalism.

EDUCATION: Now in sophomore year at New York University,
                Major in journalism, minor in art.
                Secretary of Student Council; Member of Publica-
                tions Committee and Student Art Staff.

                Graduated Boy's High School, Brooklyn, NY, June
                1988, 8th in class of 350; awarded creative
                writing medal.

                Extracurricular activities included: active
                membership in Journalism Club, Photograph Work-
                shop, Spanish Club. Library aide for three
                consecutive years.

SKILLS: Typing: 60 w.p.m.
                Good working knowledge of latest state of the art
                office machines.
                Production: page layout, mechanicals, paste-
                ups, scaling and retouching of photographs.

EMPLOYMENT: Summers, 1986, 1987: Paper route on commission
                basis.
                Summers, 1988, 1989: Apprentice at local print
                shop.

PERSONAL: Born: August 15, 1970
                Hobbies: Photo buff. Do own developing and
                printing.
                Write short stories (unpublished).

                Mother, author of series of children's books for
                Perigee Press.
                Father, well-known sports photographer.

REMARKS: Salary secondary in importance to opportunity and
                work in atmosphere of editorial department of
                large city newspaper.

PERSONAL RÉSUMÉ

JOHN S. KENLY / 100 West End Avenue, New York N.Y. / (212) 100-0000

OBJECTIVE: I am looking for a position where a person having multifarious background such as mine, can be given the opportunity to rise to the top by assuming the duties and responsibilities in line with the conspectus of qualifications outlined below.

EXPERIENCE: From 3/84 to present, serve as District Sales Manager for Ace Pharmaceuticals, located in Rahway, N.J. My responsibilities consist of directing a sales force, selling and servicing accounts among druggists, hospitals, physicians, throughout the tri-state area. I am known to be very creative in my selling and am credited with opening many new accounts with sizeable increases in sales. Assumed the position and responsibilities of District Sales Manager after two years with a salary increase commensurate with superior efforts and results. To spur on and upgrade our sales force, I have been instrumental in getting the company to set up various in-service programs which were of great help not only to our regular staff but to the additional personnel we hired to augment our sales staff. In addition I saw to it that the quality of our products was improved resulting in great expansion of sales.

From 1981 to 1984: Served as Display Supervisor with Adkay Displays, located in Long Island City, New York. My duties and responsibilities consisted in planning and supervising window display installations in drugstores throughout the greater metropolitan area, working with a team of installation specialists. Having read about silk screen printing in a trade magazine, I persuaded my company to open a silk screen department making it possible to reproduce identical displays mechanically in any desired quantity. The firm's business volume was $2,000,000 when I left the firm to take on another job. From 1977 to 1981, served as Retail Chain Store Manager for one of the New York stores owned and operated by the Robert Hall Company. Because of my obvious potentials, was within three years made manager, although I started as a humble trainee. Under my excellent supervision, our store received an award for the best decorated branch of the entire chain. This came to the attention of the owner of a firm just being organized to produce window displays for the drug and cosmetic fields, and I was offered a job with a sizable increase in salary, to become the Display Manager of the organization.

MY PERSONAL STATISTICS ARE AS FOLLOWS: I was born in Omaha, Nebraska in 3/3/55, the third son of a business manager of a chain food store in that city. There I attended Lexington Elementary School where I was graduated in 1969. When my mother remarried, after my father's death in 1970, my family moved to New York City. There I attended De Witt Clinton High School, Bronx, N.Y., graduating in 1973 with a commercial diploma. After two years service in the Army, I continued my education at Brooklyn Community College, Brooklyn, N.Y., where I was graduated with an Associate degree in Merchandising and Sales in 1977.

Other personal statistics are: Height 6'2", weight 195 lbs., eyes hazel-brown, hair prematurely gray. I am married, have two children: Johnny, age 10 and Angelina, age 7½.

I am an active member of: West Side Progressive Political Club, the local P.T.A., Red Cross Community Drive, and a number of professional organizations.

EXAMPLE OF POORLY CONSTRUCTED RÉSUMÉ
(Compare it with the one shown on opposite page.)

JOHN S. KENNY
100 West End Avenue
New York, NY 10036
(212) 100-0000

<u>OBJECTIVE:</u>	SALES EXECUTIVE for national manufacturer or distributor

<u>EXPERIENCE:</u>

1984 to Present	<u>District Sales Manager</u>, Ace Pharmaceuticals, Rahway, NY Starting as Assistant District Manager, directed staff of 12 salespeople, selling and servicing accounts among druggists, hospitals, physicians throughout the tri-state area. Initiated incentive plan resulting in 38 new accounts in highly competitive market, increasing sales volume by 45% within two years. In recognition, was promoted to District Sales Manager with a $5,000 base salary increase. Set up Dale Carnegie in-service program for continued upgrading of present force and orientation for nine new salespeople added to the staff.
1981 to 1984	<u>Display Supervisor</u>, Adkay Displays, Long Island City, NY Planned and supervised installation of drugstore displays throughout greater New York area, heading seven-man team, doing $400,000 volume of business. With company's approval, instituted silk screen facilities for printing identical displays in large quantities. This resulted in firm's entry into the syndicated display field with annual sales of $2,000,000 a year and covering New York and most New England states.
1977 to 1981	<u>Retail Chain Store Manager</u>, Stanley Hall, Inc., New York, NY Began as Trainee to become Store Manager within three years, being selected for this position over and above four others with greater seniority. Worked closely with display division in arranging interior and window displays, with our store awarded "best display" citation for entire chain. Subsequent publicity in <u>Display World</u> led to offer (at 35% salary increase) of challenging position as Display Supervisor with newly organized firm specializing in window displays for the drug and cosmetic fields.
<u>EDUCATION:</u>	<u>Graduate, Brooklyn Community College</u>, Brooklyn, NY Associate Degree in Merchandising and Sales, 1977. Professional training in Creative Selling Techniques and Personality and Human Relations, Dale Carnegie Institute.
<u>PERSONAL:</u>	Member of Art Directors' Club, Sales Executive Club, American Management Association, Vice President, P.T.A.

THOMAS R. REILLY
100 Marcy Place
Katonah, New York 10006
(914) 100-0000

Age 44 - Height 5'11" - Weight 165 lbs. - Married - Top physical condition

---

SEEK ADMINISTRATIVE POSITION IN INDUSTRIAL RELATIONS FIELD UTILIZING MILITARY EXPERIENCE AND EDUCATION BACKGROUND.

EDUCATION:

B.S. degree, LeMoyne College, Syracuse, New York, June 1967
Major - Industrial Relations; Minor - Economics
3.43 (4-point scale) average; top 5% of class.

Honors - 4-year Academic Scholarship; Who's Who--
Dean's List; Industrial Relations Medal; Dorm Proctor.

Extracurricular Activities: Senior Senator in Student Government; Class President, Junior Year; Student Appeals Court Justice; Manager, Soccer Team.

MILITARY HISTORY:

Career Officer. Graduate, Air Force Officer Training School, 1968. Served as manpower and organization consultant to top level management, Air Defense Command, Colorado; intermediate staff, 9th Aerospace Defense Division, Colorado; base operative level, Korat AB, Thailand, SEA.

Service Experience Directly Related to Industrial Relations

- Conducted surveys on effective personnel utilization.
- Engaged in planning, establishing, streamlining phases of new aerospace programs.
- Effected savings of over $350,000 through a study of grade and skill requirements of missile unit of over 400 personnel. Received special letter of commendation.
- Planned organizational structures for all management levels.
- Headed a SEA manpower and organization team that provided managerial services to combative and supportive units, manned by over 5,000 personnel.

INTERESTS AND HOBBIES:

Extensive reading--mostly on economics and American labor movement. Swimming, golf, tennis, as time permits.

MARY BRUCE WINTER
100 East 74th Street
New York, NY 10021
(212) 100-0000

FORMER LEGAL SECRETARY, NOW 45-YEAR-OLD HOUSEWIFE
WITH TWO CHILDREN OFF AT COLLEGE, SEEKS POSITION AS
LIBRARY RESEARCH ASSISTANT IN COLLEGE OR PROFESSIONAL
LIBRARY, ON A PART-TIME BASIS.

EDUCATION:

Formal education included completion of two-year liberal
arts program at Endicott Junior College, Beverly, MA,
graduating with Associate of Arts degree. This was followed
up with office and secretarial training at Gibbs Secretarial
School in New York City.

WORK EXPERIENCE:

Prior to marriage in 1968, was employed in one-girl office
of John Haberman, a New York City patent attorney. In
addition to general secretarial work--typing, stenography,
bookkeeping, correspondence--50% of my time was taken up
assisting my employer with research projects, including
visits to public as well as professional law libraries.
It was this phase of my job that I enjoyed best.

TIME AVAILABILITY:

Though my preference is for a ten-to-three work day, I will
be glad to consider flexibility in work schedule to suit
time requirements of the job.

PERSONAL:

In best of health - 20/20 vision

Am avid reader, enjoy outdoor sports and active
participation in community welfare organizations.

Husband is practicing architect employed by Skidmore, Owings
& Merrill, New York.

REFERENCES AVAILABLE

RENEE SMITH
100 Merrick Place
Garden City, NY 11211
(516) 100-0000

POSITION DESIRED: PARALEGAL/ADMINISTRATIVE ASSISTANT for Major Law Firm.

EDUCATION: New York University, New York (1986-1988)
32 credits in business administration.

Pace College, New York (1985-1986)
Completed Paralegal/Legal Assistant Program.

Andrew Jackson High School, New York (1981-1985)
Major in secretarial and business practice.

EMPLOYMENT: Paralegal and Administrative Assistant
Law offices of Ronald P. Murphy, Esq.
201 Main Street, Valley Stream, NY
Specialist in Corporation Law.

1986 to date   Started as Legal Secretary. Within a year, was promoted to Administrative Assistant in charge of office staff of three, with salary increment of $1,500. Reason for desiring change: Happy in my job, but would like to work in mid-Manhattan, close to Hunter College, where I hope to continue my education in the evening to complete credit requirements for bachelor's degree.

1985 to 1986   Legal Secretary
Law offices of Harry Katzman, Esq., 500 Fifth Avenue, New York. General law practice.

Summer 1985   Secretarial Assistant
Law office of ex-Supreme Court Justice Sternberg, 185 Madison Avenue, New York.

PERSONAL: Single; attractive; perfect health; 5'5", 115 lbs.

Aspire to achieve professional level of attorney.

SALARY: Negotiable.

MILDRED MORENO
100 Brookline Street
Hartford, CT 07612
(614) 100-0000

TOP-NOTCH SECRETARY * BOOKKEEPER * TYPIST * RECEPTIONIST

seeks relocation in Boston area to permit her
to continue her education at Boston University.

EXPERIENCE:

1989/date	J.P. Henley & Company Financial Underwriters Hartford, CT	Secretary to loan administrator. Handle cash disbursements, credit and processing of loans. Do reports and own correspondence from hastily dictated notes. Supervise 2 typists and 1 clerk.
1986/1989	Sterling Crafters, Inc. Custom-made lampshades Hartford, CT	Secretary, receptionist, bookkeeper. One gal office. Duties involved payroll for 14 employees, cash receipts. Assisted with advertising campaigns.
1984/1986	Clarion Enterprises Music Publishers Hartford, CT	In charge of accounts receivable, made bank deposits, used Friden Key-Punch, adding machine. Served as secretary to account executive, doing own and major portion of her correspondence.

EDUCATION:

Graduate, Central Community College, Norwalk, CT, June 1984.
On Dean's List for two years.

Projected educational plans include evening study toward B.S.
degree in Business Administration.

PERSONAL:

Age 26; 5'4"; 121 lbs; excellent health.

SYLVIA ROTH
100 Riverside Drive
New York, N.Y. 10001
(212) 100-0000

<u>OBJECTIVE</u>:	Administrative Assistant to busy Executive.
<u>QUALIFICATIONS AND EXPERIENCE</u>:	Best expressed in the words of an ad my immediate supervisor placed in the classified section of Women's Wear Daily, upon my giving notice that I intend to resign as soon as he can find a replacement.

> <u>"I am losing my Best Girl. She types like a dream, takes dictation faster than I can talk, handles clients with tact and diplomacy, does library research, thinks, works under pressure, and SMILES."</u>

My total work experience since finishing college has been with <u>Smithline Associates</u>, 385 Madison Avenue, New York City--a fashion advertising agency employing 30 people. After 5 years, I plan to leave under most amicable conditions to diversify my experience in area of administration and management.

<u>EDUCATION</u>:

<u>Pace College</u>, New York, N.Y. 1983-1985
A.A. degree in Secretarial Studies.

<u>High School of Art & Design</u>, New York, N.Y. 1979-1983
A Average. Punctuality and Attendance Award.

<u>PERSONAL</u>:

Born August 11, 1965; Height 5'5"; Weight 122 lbs.
Appearance: well groomed; considered attractive.
Happy outlook on life.

<u>AFFILIATIONS</u>:

Corresponding Secretary, Advertising Club of N.Y.
Member, Advertising Women's Production Club.
Member, Promotion Committee, local chapter, YWCA.

<u>REFERENCES</u>:

My present employer:
Mr. Edward R. Smithline, President
Smithline Associates
385 Madison Avenue, New York, N.Y.

Jane Mazur
100 Green Street
Bronx, New York 10468

RECEPTIONIST WHO NOT ONLY SMILES BUT WORKS

POSITION SOUGHT:
Receptionist in executive office of large corporation, preferably in mid-town Manhattan.

EDUCATION:
Honor graduate, Walton High School, Bronx, New York, June 1987.

Courses included:
- Speed Typing
- Office Practice
- Word Processing
- Secretarial Sciences
- Office Machines
- Creative Writing
- Business Math
- Speech

EXPERIENCE:
From June 1987 to present, act as assistant to Ms. Mary Rice, Manager, Claims Department, Alexander's, Bronx, New York. Wish to leave to attend Hunter College (evening session) with a view of continuing my education towards a B.S. degree.

During summer months of '85 and '86, served as assistant to Indexer in Editorial Department, Chelsea Publishing Co., New York.

PERSONAL:
Excellent health; 5'7", 122 lbs.; single. Hobbies include jogging, swimming, off-Broadway theater, and window shopping.

REFERENCES:
My present supervisor, Ms. Mary Rice, who knows of my intentions for leaving, will gladly substantiate my work record via phone 933-1000, or by mail: Ms. Mary Rice, Supervisor, Claims Department, Alexander's, Bronx, New York 10467.

ARNOLD KAFFEN   100 Main Street, Stanford, CT 06902, (203) 100-0000

CERTIFIED PUBLIC ACCOUNTANT

CAREER HISTORY:

| 1978-Present | ARTHUR YOUNG & COMPANY |
| | An International Firm of Certified Public Accountants. |

Audit Manager	-	**Stanford**	(9/87 - Present)
	-	**Paris**	(9/84 - 8/87)
	-	**New York**	(1/78 - 6/84)

Staff Assistant, Senior Accountant, Supervisor - New York (1/78 - 6/84)

Responsible for auditing and diverse financial, operational and ongoing advisory services to multinational corporations.

Director of Accounting and Auditing - Paris (9/84 - 8/87)

Responsible for the office's auditing, accounting and financial reporting, including establishing and maintaining effective internal controls to ensure quality of work and adherence to policies and procedures and guiding 75 professionals in correctly applying U.S. and European professional standards.

Industry experience includes manufacturing (wire and cable, consumer products, electronic components, precision timepieces, heavy machinery, shipbuilding, textile products), oil and gas, import/export, publishing, real estate, financial services, insurance, entertainment, legal services, etc.

Representative experience includes the following:

Administration

- Planned, budgeted and controlled audit work on five continents, directing up to 25 managers and other professionals at multi-locations.

- Administered a 20-person accounting and auditing support function.

- Directed company employees such as internal auditors, accounting department personnel and analysts performing audit-related work.

Planning

- Prepared and implemented the Paris office's annual Action Plan.

Budgeting

- Developed a corporation's multi-divisional six-month operating budget.

Billing and Collection

- Managed receivables, established billing terms, forecasted cash flows and recommended adjustments and write-offs.

EDP

- Developed EDP recommendations and consulted on implementation.

- Guided management in centralizing and computerizing its accounting.

ARNOLD KAFFEN . . . Page 2

Cost Accounting	• Reviewed cost accounting and inventory systems at plants, analyzed the data (including variances) generated by these systems and recommended system improvements.
Analytical/ Financial	• Employed budget/actual comparisons and ratio and trend analysis to identify items requiring follow-up.
	• Performed acquisition reviews, lease versus purchase studies, reviews of property insurance coverage, compliance with loan agreements, etc.
	• Reviewed contracts and extracted relevant financial information.
Accounting	• Consulted with financial executives on the impact of completed or contemplated transactions and of new professional and SEC pronouncements.
	• Standardized the consolidation of a $4 billion diversified corporation and trained corporate accounting personnel to perform the mechanics.
Tax	• Prepared or reviewed complex book/tax reconciliations.
	• Reviewed tax returns for consistency with the financial statements.
SEC/Financial Reporting	• Prepared or reviewed annual and interim financial statements for management, shareholders and the SEC.
	• Conducted technical reviews of diverse SEC filings and financial statements in the New York Report Review Department.
	• Directed the review of financial statements prepared under U.S. and diverse European accounting principles.
Management Reporting	• Recommended ways to improve profitability, efficiency and controls in reports to top management and Audit Committees.
EDUCATION:	• MBA with distinction (first in class), Syracuse University - 1978 Finance and Quantitative Methods
	• BS, University of Maryland - 1976 Accounting
PROFESSIONAL:	• American Institute of Certified Public Accountants • New York State and Connecticut Societies of CPA's
COMMUNITY:	• Advisor, Junior Achievement • Area Coordinator, United Way
LANGUAGE:	• Fluent in French

VICKI MENDEZ
100 38th Street
Woodside, New York 11310
(212) 100-0000

CAREER OBJECTIVE

Executive Position in Personnel Management involving major supervisory and administrative responsibilities.

SYNOPSIS

College graduate with degree in Personnel Management. Major courses include: Personnel Interviewing, Industrial Psychology, Psychological Testing, Human Relations, Management Training, Labor Laws.

Diversified business experience in office procedures involving: office supervision of personnel, liaison with executive staff, preparation of reports and office memoranda, correspondence.

WORK EXPERIENCE

Metropolitan Container Corp., New York City

1983
to
Present

As Executive Secretary to the Sales Manager of the Corrugated Container Division, have varied responsibilities ranging from the customary secretarial duties to charge of the Sales Manager's office in his absence, involving some independent decision authority.

Responsibilities encompass (in addition to the usual office activities and procedures) decision authorization on matters of price quotations, information on product line, customer inquiries concerning shipment and special orders.

Deal directly with VIP's from parent and other companies, handling travel and transportation arrangements, hotel reservations, scheduling attendance at meetings.

Draft monthly reports on the division's sales volume for presentation to audit department. Handle most of Sales Manager's business correspondence and records.

Credited with introducing a computerized filing system which proved to be so effective that it was adopted by other divisions of the company.

Red Star Oil Company, Inc., New York City

1978
to
1983

As <u>Secretary</u> to the Manager of Technical Publications, had diversified duties beyond the usual secretarial responsibilities, including arranging of conferences, direct dealings with staff members on various levels and editorial assignments.

Responsible for editing and proofreading of copy for technical publications, inter-office bulletins and newsletters and arranging for printing and distribution.

Composed own correspondence to both domestic and foreign field representatives.

Directed the activities of two stenotypists assigned to our office.

EDUCATION

<u>New York University</u>, School of Commerce, 1984-1989
B.S. in Personnel Management, June 1989 (evening session)

<u>Dale Carnegie Institute</u>, New York, February-April 1983
Effective Speaking and Human Relations

<u>Berkeley Business School</u>, New York, February-August 1978
Completed intensified secretarial course

<u>Central Commercial High School</u>, New York, 1973-1977
Graduated with honors, 10th in class of 340

PERSONAL DATA

Born: April 3, 1960   Health: excellent
Height: 5'5"   Marital Status: single
Weight: 119 lbs.   Finances: no debts, own car

Hobbies: Crossword puzzle buff, foreign films, tennis
Language Skill: Spanish, Arabic, French

REFERENCES

Excellent references readily available.

LOUIS K. BRAND
100 Delaware Avenue
Washington, D.C. 20000
(301) 100-0000

OBJECTIVE:

INTERNATIONAL TRAFFIC MANAGER, with goal of becoming increasingly identified with international operations management; sales and marketing; planning, implementing methods and controls to develop and improve operations.

SUMMARY OF BACKGROUND:

Sixteen years diversified and increasingly responsible traffic management experience. Have consistently demonstrated a practical, yet imaginative, approach to management responsibilities--always interested in seeking new ways to do things better, faster and more economically. Successful in building efficiency through the introduction of systems, methods and controls that get the desired results. Have been effective in supervising and coordinating personnel, maintaining high esprit-de-corps.

EXPERIENCE:

1982-date

U.S. Government, Washington, D.C.
Traffic Management Specialist
. . . Establish regional operations for handling AID shipments to Africa and the Middle East. Currently engaged in the coordination of world-wide export shipments through contact with GSA regional offices, government agencies and transportation companies.

1976-1982

Smith Kline & French Laboratories, Philadelphia, Pa.
Assistant International Traffic Manager
. . . Helped expedite traffic department through improved business systems and effective use of personnel.

1974-1976

Pan American World Airways, San Juan, Puerto Rico
Assistant Station Cargo Manager
. . . Administration of office functions including handling of majority of correspondence and claims; supervised use of accounting procedures; worked closely with cargo manager on matters of policy.

1970-1974

United States Lines Co., Boston, Mass.
Freight Representative
. . . Began as assistant in export department...then in charge of steamship operations customs, purchasing, preparation of governmental statistical reports...promoted to position of Freight Representative.

SUMMARY OF ACHIEVEMENTS:

Systems & Methods	Designed carbon inter-leaf forms using maximum amount of pre-printed data; used master forms for replacing multi-sheet invoices as a time saver. After a six-month study (jointly with company's Systems and Procedures Department), a completely automatic invoicing system was designed to further increase the efficiency of the department.
Planning	Established priorities in clerical work with overall organization benefit in mind. Scheduled shipments to be consistent with personnel workloads. Assisted department head in making personnel forecasts, planning for average rather than peak loads. Planned shipments to foreign plants, where timing and cost factors were most vital.
Analyzing Situations	Displayed in various ways an ability to analyze company departmental goals and come up with a workable solution. Solutions were both corrective and preventive as the problem presented itself. One corrective solution resulted in 30% increase in orders, introduced labor-saving devices which reduced shipping delays by over 50% and, at the same time, held down requirements for personnel increases.
Personnel Handling	Supervised 30 people. Assumed responsibility of office management during transition period between changes in managers. Reviewed applications and conducted interviews of applicants by the personnel department. Assisted department head at semi-annual reviews of job performance, and made recommendations for salary increases.
Liaison	Responsible for liaison between employer and outside organizations including sales representatives and others on sales-service administrative problems, invoices and payments; insurance companies relative to rates and service, and government agencies on details relating to licenses and shipments. Responsible for liaison coordination with accounting department in regard to banking documents, systems and procedures, office layouts for department manpower.

EDUCATION: Georgetown University, Washington, D.C.
B.F.S. degree (Shipping Major), June 1970.

SALARY: Negotiable.

PERSONAL DATA: Age 38; happily married, 3 sons.

ROY O'HARA
100 Kent Avenue
Trenton, N.J. 08000
(609) 100-0000

DIRECTOR OF PURCHASING

with top-level experience in effective vendor relationships to buy at lowest cost without sacrifice in service or quality. Versatile background in interrelated fields in purchasing, accounting and selling.

EXPERIENCE:

1986/date   <u>PURCHASING MANAGER</u>, stationery and printing; Milk and Cream Division, Sunshine Dairy Products, Hershey, Pa. Purchasing offices in Trenton, N.J.

The purchasing budget of my department runs in excess of $5 million annually. Of this, approximately 18% is in office supplies and interoffice printing; 82% in dealer-aid promotion-- window and counter displays, posters, display stands, shelf talkers, etc.

- Because of thorough working knowledge of major printing processes (letterpress, offset, photogelatine and silk screen), am able to properly evaluate technical aspects of printed matter from the point of view of vendor's production costs and quality of finished product.
- Have stimulated vendor competition through fair and equal treatment to all with result that company prestige among suppliers and vendors is highest in company's 25-year history.
- Have initiated system of thorough investigation of vendor's position in the field in terms of production facilities and management. Failures of vendors to make scheduled deliveries have been cut by 75%.
- Have instituted procedures for awarding orders based on sealed competitive bidding, resulting in savings of more than $350,000 annually.
- Attend production clinics, demonstration and trade shows to keep abreast with latest technical developments, to broaden scope of new supply and merchandising innovations. Read major trade journals which have a bearing on purchasing, manufacture and line of company products.

1980/1986   ASSISTANT PURCHASING DIRECTOR, Ranther Company, Inc., Jersey City, N.J. Manufacturers of electronic units for the communications industry. Company employs 750 people.

         - Began as Junior Purchasing Agent, then advanced to Assistant Purchasing Director with substantial salary increase.
         - Successfully expedited orders to maintain flow of material to meet rigid production schedules at cost below 20% of that of my predecessor, with highest quality of performance.
         - Gross income-profit ratio more than doubled during my six years with the company. Letter of commendation by President of the company paid tribute to my ability. Bonus of $3,500 check accompanied the letter.

1975/1980   DISTRICT SALESMAN, Snow Crop Foods, Inc., New York. Food Processors, employing 255 people.

         - Contacted chain and retail food outlets in central New Jersey. Promoted to chain contact man with responsibility to one of the large metropolitan New York chain organizations. Was top salesperson among 18, with highest record of sales. Was selected to organize sales and distribution functions with three jobbers, increasing major outlets by 35%, with value of sales increase over 120%.

EDUCATION: Rutgers University, New·Brunswick, N.J., 1971-1975.
         B.S. degree. Major in Business Management.
Fairleigh Dickinson University, Rutherford, N.J.
         Graduate course in Sales and Merchandising.

PERSONAL: Age 37; Height 5'11"; Weight 183 lbs; Good health
Married, 2 children; U.S. Citizen
Own home and late-model car
Member, National Association of Purchasing Agents

SALARY: To be discussed in personal interview.

REFERENCES: Business, bank and personal references on request.

JUAN ORTIZ   100 Main Street, Dayton, OH 44311   (513) 100-0000

<u>PRINTING TECHNICIAN</u>

GENERAL MANAGER, COMMERCIAL PRINTING PLANT;
CAPTIVE PRINTING AND/OR MAILING FACILITY

SUMMARY OF
EXPERIENCE

<u>1985 - Date</u>: MANAGER, PRODUCTION DEPARTMENT,
with one of nation's most prestigious rate
tariff bureaus.

Supervise staff of 23. Responsible for
production of 50 million pages of tariff
material each year plus all bulletins, dockets,
miscellaneous forms and office copies. Mail 65
million pages per year to 9,500 subscribers who
receive all possible combinations of 31 separate
publications. Maintain mailing lists and
subscription changes, new orders, inventories,
warehouse operations.

Accomplishments: Effected annual savings in
printing production costs in first 14 months on
job; lowered production cost per page from .005
to .003; handled additional 1.8 million pages
per month with a 36% savings over outside
vendors' costs; increased production by over 60%
without additions to staff; effected $2,100
monthly postage savings through installation of
computer to sort address lists into zip code
order for bulk rate mailing.

<u>1984 - 1985</u>: Ohio University, Athens, OH;
Department of Office Services.

Involved in a one-year study of methods of
operation in institutional captive printing
plant. Published recommendations which formed
the basis for reorganization of Addressograph
Department.

<u>1980 - 1984</u>: HEAD, OFFSET DEPARTMENT, Reynolds
Premium Printing Company, Akron, OH.

Reorganized Offset Department. Complete
departmental responsibility for production and
sales; planning and directing work of 25
employees; preparation of printed items from
copy to finished proof; estimating job costs.

<u>1978 - 1980</u>: SALES PROMOTION, SALES TRAINEE, Falco Paper Company, Sandusky, OH.

Served 3 house accounts. Technical troubleshooter on paper problems encountered by printers and lithographers.

TECHNICAL SKILLS	<u>WORKING KNOWLEDGE OF FOLLOWING</u>: <u>Desk-top Publishing</u>: Apple Macintosh, IBM-based desk-top printer, Compugraphic photo typesetting equipment. <u>Presses</u>: Hamada 600, 700, 800; Ryobi 2800, 3200; A.B. Dick 2024; Davidson 241. <u>Cameras</u>: Itek 1218, Ektalith, Xerox, NuArc, Mitsubishi, Silvermaster, stripping, plate making, opaquing. <u>Bindery</u>: Macey 12-station collator, Thomas Rotomatic Collator, A & M rotary sorter, Baum folder, Rosback 6-station signature inserter, Rosback 3-station signature inserter with saddle stitcher, Myriad drill, Lawson drill, Challenge cutters.
EDUCATION AND TRAINING	<u>Graduate</u>, Central High School, Cleveland, OH. <u>Graduate</u>, Printing Apprenticeship Program. <u>Completed</u> 6-month evening course, company training program in Sales Promotion. <u>Graduate</u>, A.A. degree, Cleveland Community College.
MEMBERSHIP	Production Men's Club; National Typographic Society; Advisory Committee, Vocational Training, Board of Education.
PERSONAL	Born........5/1/58 Health........Excellent Height...... 5'8" Married......2 children Weight....169 lbs. Finances..In good order
OUTSIDE INTERESTS	Technical literature. Collecting first editions. Fishing, golf and gardening, as time permits.

<u>LETTERS OF COMMENDATION AND REFERENCES AVAILABLE UPON REQUEST.</u>

THEODORE KOENIG
100 Loganville Road
Oakland, Calif. 91502
(213) 100-0000

MARKETING-SALES MANAGEMENT

More than 10 years in marketing and sales management with national and regional organizations, including new product development, advertising and distribution. Experience acquired while serving with:

Fleming Drug Corp., Oakland, Calif.
National Foods, Inc., St. Paul, Minn.

- **OPERATIONS MANAGEMENT**
  1987-date.   As **Manager of Operations** with Fleming Drug Corp., Pharmaceutical Division, have supervisory authority for marketing, production, distribution and accounting, with production facilities located throughout the United States and Canada.   Responsible for the introduction and development of a computer program to provide effective inventory controls.   Achieved efficiency savings of more than $175,000 during the first year of operation.

- **PRODUCT DEVELOPMENT**
  1985-1987.   As **Product Manager** with Fleming Drug Corp., was instrumental in initiating several new household products, resulting in highest margin of profits in company line. This was accomplished through coordination of research, production, highly effective promotional program and new packaging concepts.

- **MARKETING AND SALES**
  1983-1985.   As **Regional Sales Manager** with Fleming Drug Corp., my territory comprised central U.S.A. (approximately 14 states).   Supervised a total of 53 brokers and sales personnel. Effected 60% increase in sales through special marketing programs and developed "spot" systems, resulting in better customer distribution at lower costs. Acknowledged as "The Regional Manager able to achieve highest sales objectives with minimum expenditures."

1982-1983. As **District Manager** with Fleming Drug Corp., my territory comprised five states. Increased sales 22% the first year in a highly competitive market. Moved up to position as Regional Sales Manager.

1979-1982. As **Wholesale Sales Representative** with National Foods, Inc., early career experience was in selling to wholesalers and chain stores in a three-state area. Opened 18 new accounts which previous sales representatives had not been able to reach.

- **OTHER ACHIEVEMENTS**
  Consultant for major banking institution, analyzing marketing problems of small companies.
  Inventor of closure devices and several product efficiency tools.
  Feature writer for a number of trade journals including the Food Processor, Drug Trade Monthly and Scientific American.
  Recipient of Public Speaking Awards.

- **EDUCATION**
  Graduate, University of Wisconsin, B.S. degree, 1979.
  Major in General Business, minor in Finance.

  Special courses in Industrial Management and Computerization at: Bradley University Graduate School; Louis A. Allen Management School; IBM School.

- **PERSONAL**
  Age 33, 5'11", 175 lbs. Good health. Married, two children.
  Active in tennis, racquetball and softball.
  Avid reader of business books and journals.

- **AFFILIATIONS**
  American Management Association
  Board of Directors, YMCA
  Executive Club of Oakland Chamber of Commerce

Portfolio of records available.

LYNN ROBINS
100 Illinois Avenue
Norwalk, CT 07000
(714) 100-0000

JOB OBJECTIVE:

To begin as <u>MARKETING MANAGEMENT TRAINEE</u>, with opportunity to advance to account executive level.

EDUCATION:

<u>B.S. degree, 1990; Cornell University</u>, Ithaca, NY.
Major in Economics; minor in Psychology.
B+ average in both subject fields.

Tuition financed 60% through summer jobs; 40% through Connecticut State Scholarship. Plan to continue graduate work towards Master's degree in Marketing and Management at the University of Connecticut, evening division.

<u>Graduate, 1986; Central High School</u>, Norwalk, CT.
Business manager and chief ad solicitor for student publications.
Member of debating team, service squad, student council. President of senior class.

WORK EXPERIENCE:

<u>Production Assistant</u> (Media Department)	-----------------	Summer of 1989
Harris-Gray Advertising Agency		
<u>Survey Interviewer</u>	--------------------------------------	Summer of 1988
National Broadcasting Corp.		
<u>Assistant Bookkeeper</u>	--------------------------------------	Summer of 1987
French-American Banking Corp.		
<u>Door-to-door selling</u>	--------------------------------------	Summer of 1986
Encyclopaedia Britannica		

PERSONAL:

Enjoy reading. Follow stock market reports (a non-investor).
Subscribe to Wall Street Journal, Business Week.

REFERENCES ON HAND

OBJECTIVE	POSITION AS MANAGER FOR INTERNATIONAL BANKING FIRM

EXPERIENCE   AMERICAN BANKING INTERNATIONAL, MIAMI, FLORIDA

Aug. 1987   International Personal Banking Assistant.
   to   Responsibilities include all phases of contact-
Present   area activities related to opening and servicing
                  current savings accounts, loan extensions to
                  individual customers, overdraft authorization,
                  quoting and establishing domestic and eurodollar
                  time deposits, and personalized attention to
                  customers' wide range of international banking
                  needs.

                  Direct correspondence with customers, both in
                  English and Spanish. Responsible for all domestic
                  and international credit investigations and
                  inquiries.

Jan. 1987   AMERICAN BANKING INTERNATIONAL, CHICAGO, ILLINOIS
   to
Aug. 1987   Executive Secretary. Latin-American Division.
                  Transferred to Miami to assist in opening the
                  Florida branch and become a member of the staff.

1984   HELENE CURTIS INTERNATIONAL, CHICAGO, ILLINOIS
   to
1987   Executive Secretary. Assistant to Executive Vice
                  President, Latin-American Division.

1979   TRIAD EXPORT COMPANY, TRENTON, INDIANA
   to
1984   Translator. English, Spanish and French.
                  Correspondence, technical bulletins, brochures and
                  advertising material.

EDUCATION   Villanova Univ., Havana, Cuba (B.A. Economics)
                  Havana Univ., Havana, Cuba (School of Languages)
                  L'Alliance Francaise, Havana, Cuba (French)
                  American Institute of Banking, Chicago, Illinois

ADDITIONAL   U.S. Citizen. Fluent in English, Spanish, French.
DATA   Working knowledge of Portuguese and Italian.

RICHARD M. CONNOLLY
000 Crotona Avenue
Sacramento, CA 90000
(213) 100-0000

OFFERING OVER 15 YEARS EXPERIENCE IN INDUSTRIAL MANAGEMENT WITH RECORD FOR LOWERING PRODUCTION COSTS AND INCREASING COMPANY PROFITS

EXPERIENCE:

<u>GENERAL MANAGER</u>, reporting to President.
    The Wilson Corporation, Sacramento, CA.
    (Food processors; sales volume $14 million.)

1984-Date

Started as Assistant Manager. Worked out a highly successful program of cost control. This resulted in a 38% savings in manufacturing costs, as well as in sales and operating overhead. Was moved up to position as General Manager with complete charge of all operations in 1986. Plant capacity has been doubled and five new branches opened, with company profits rising to an all-time high.

<u>OFFICE MANAGER</u>, reporting to General Manager.
    Johnson Drug Corporation, Sandusky, OH.
    (Pharmaceutical specialties; sales volume $4 million.)

1981-1984

Started as bookkeeper and accountant in 1981. Because of success in instituting a 30% savings in branch office and warehouse overhead, was made Office Manager in 1983, from which position voluntarily resigned the following year to accept an attractive offer from the Wilson Corporation.

<u>ASSISTANT WORKS MANAGER</u>, reporting to Works Manager.
    Royal Corrugated Container Corp., Sandusky, OH.
    (Shipped cartons for the food packaging industry.)

1975-1981

Started as head of Receiving Department; transferred to Planning Division in 1977. Six months later, was placed in charge of all clerical work in the department. Suggested changes in routing which resulted in salvaging 15% of production waste of paper and board, with a saving of over $65,000 annually. In 1980, was made Assistant to the Works Manager in charge of production. Preferring office management work as a career, resigned to accept position with the Johnson Drug Corporation.

EDUCATION:

<u>Southern Louisiana College</u>, Hammond, LA
    B.A. in Business Administration, 1975.
<u>Dale Carnegie Institute</u>, Sandusky, OH
    15-week course in Dynamics of Human Relations, 1977.
<u>International Correspondence School</u>, Minneapolis, MN
    Completed correspondence course in Accounting, 1980.

AVOCATIONAL INTERESTS:

Hobbies: Golf, fishing, camping. Avid reader, mostly biographies and books on economics.

CALLIGRAPHIC ARTIST & DESIGNER READY TO WORK FOR YOU ON A FREELANCE BASIS

FORMAL ART TRAINING:

High School of Music & Art, New York. Graduate.
  Honor student; Winner of the Alexander medal.

Pratt Institute, New York
  Completed two-year course in graphic design
  with emphasis on calligraphic lettering.

ADDITIONAL STUDY:

Attended two workshop seminars in calligraphy
under Arnold Bank and Arthur Baker, both
world renowned calligraphic designers.

PROFESSIONAL AFFILIATIONS:

Society of Scribes
Typophiles of America
American Institute of Graphic Art.

PERSONAL:

A serious automobile accident seven years ago
left me paralyzed from the waist down, thus making
it unpractical for me to keep my position as staff artist
with the Delphi Design Studios, located in Newark, N.J.
Have therefore set up a home studio, specializing in:

- PROCLAMATIONS AND CITATIONS
- SCHOOL DIPLOMAS AND CERTIFICATES
- INVITATIONS FOR SPECIAL OCCASIONS
- HAND-LETTERING FOR REPRODUCTION

I can arrange for pick-up and delivery of all work

JANE GLICKSMAN

100 East 74th St. New York, N.Y. 10028 Phone (212) 100-0000

DON O'CONNOR, JR.
100 Cordtlandt Street
Philadelphia, PA 41000
(721) 100-0000

OBJECTIVE: *Editor-in-chief with large New York publishing firm, specializing in textbooks and programmed information.*

SUMMARY: *Fifteen years experience as high school teacher and editor. Proven ability to work closely with authors: contract negotiations, guidance in manuscript preparation, production and promotion. Seek to relocate in New York area to expand professional horizons beyond present scope.*

EDITORIAL
EXPERIENCE: Managing Editor *of a small but highly prestigious Philadelphia book publisher.*

1983-Date   *Work entails all phases of book production and supervision of a staff of three junior editors and two readers. Through personal contact with schools and knowledge of curriculum structure, have initiated new department in programmed workbooks--a venture which has boosted gross annual sales by 35% on a profit margin considerably above the average return.*

1979-1983   Assistant Editor *with Hallmark Press, a limited editions publisher in Erie, PA.*

Responsibilities included reading of authors' manuscripts, mark-up of copy and proofreading. Liaison between editorial, art and production departments.

TEACHING
EXPERIENCE: *Taught English and Social Studies in Philadelphia public school system. Special interest and training in course-of-study evaluation, visual aids and curriculum construction. Faculty adviser, student publications.*

1974-1979

EDUCATION: M.A. degree (Journalism), *New York University, NY, 1974.* B.S. degree, *Temple University, Philadelphia, PA, 1973.*

AVOCATIONAL
INTERESTS: *Typophile (own and operate small hand press). Short story writing, painting, horseback riding, photography.*

MARY D. AVONNE
100 East 4th Street
New York, N.Y. 10000
(212) 100-0000

** **

<u>WORK HISTORY</u>:	Diversified experience as staff art director, art editor, free-lance designer and illustrator, both in the United States and abroad.
(Abroad) 1978-1990	<u>Art Director</u>: Havas Consel Publicité, Paris, France. Responsibilities included staff supervision and direction; purchasing outside art services for choice accounts such as Charles Jourdan Shoes, Evian Water, Cointreau Liqueur, De Beers Consolidated Mines, Sanforized Label, Moet and Chandon Champagne, L'Oréal.
	<u>Consultant</u>: Gray Advertising, Buenos Aires, Argentina. Variety of special assignments in illustration, layout, photography, graphics, and promotional concepts.
(In the States) 1974-1978	<u>Executive Art Director</u>: Atlas Advertising, New York, N.Y. Layout design, supervising three assistants, client contact, selection and supervision of photography and type, idea formulation with copy staff.
	<u>Art Director</u>: Gray Advertising, New York, N.Y. Advertising concepts, layout and illustration for choice accounts such as Cutex, Coty's, Pond's, Skol Suntan Lotion.
	<u>Assistant Art Director</u>: Kenyon and Eckhardt, New York, N.Y.
	<u>Staff Artist</u>: Batten, Barton, Durstine & Osborne, New York, N.Y.
<u>EDUCATION</u> <u>& TRAINING</u>:	Académie de la Grande Chaumière, Paris, France; 1983-1987 New School for Social Research, New York, N.Y.; 1973-1977 The Art Students League, New York, N.Y. 1970-1973
<u>PERSONAL</u>	Mother of 2 teenagers; U.S. citizen; fluent in French and Spanish. Desire to remain in my native country (U.S.A.) to give my family a feeling of permanence and stability, and take part in civic affairs and community life.

Mary D. Avonne

100 KENNEDY DRIVE   ST. LOUIS, MO 80000   (815) 100-0000

JOURNALIST / PHOTOGRAPHER

Special assignments for dynamic publishing company: field interview research, non-fiction articles and books, including photography when needed.

EDUCATIONAL BACKGROUND:

M.A. in Journalism, Jan. 1987, University of Missouri.
Named the outstanding student and most able writer among 400 at the University of Missouri School of Journalism, in 1986. Earned 3.6 grade average of 4.0 system. In top 5% of class. Major work in magazine-feature writing and photography. Advanced graduate work in non-fiction writing, feature stories, reporting, press photography, picture editing.
Member, Sigma Delta Chi, national professional journalism society; Kappa Tau Alpha, national scholastic honorary for journalism students. Officer, Kappa Alpha Mu, national honorary photo-journalism fraternity; Representative, Journalism Student's Association. Recipient of "Reader's Digest" award for feature article writing.

B.S. degree, June 1983, Purdue University.
Citation as Distinguished Student and Distinguished Military Graduate. Earned 5.0 on 6.0 grade system. Emphasis on accelerated writing courses and economics.
Member, Phi Eta Sigma scholastic honorary; Honor Key recipient (four times); Dean's List. Served on campus magazine and ROTC publications staffs. Residence social chairman for four years. Campus radio station announcer. College expenses financed through high school savings and extensive part-time work.

EXPERIENCE:

Have written more than 150 full-length feature articles in addition to numerous research and report assignments. More than 1,000 photos in print. Have traveled some 30,000 miles in pursuing feature material. Copies of articles in print now exceed 11 million. Article subjects range from auto safety, business management, camping and economics through retarded children, supermarkets, travel, used car buying and workshops.

Reporter and feature writer on the "Columbia Missourian," daily--Sunday paper with circulation of 50,000. Covered numerous feature assignments, police and fire beats, hospitals, elections, accidents. More than 20 major features published in addition to six-day-a-week 'hard news' pieces over several months. Many full page photo feature stories and numerous single photos.

Editor-in-Charge for "Chain Store Age Magazine," a 150-page monthly with 60,000 paid circulation. Interviewed corporate presidents, executives, financiers and managers. During initial six months with company, gathered information, took pictures for, and wrote more than 20 major articles, edited seven, and contributed to 15 other works for publication and publicity, with an aggregate total of 55 published pages. Also shot some 2,000 pictures, many in color.

Field Editor and Writer-Photographer for "Super Service Station Magazine," a 200-page trade monthly with an international circulation of 120,000. Left position for graduate work and advanced degree in journalism. Returned at full pay during 1987, covered 10 states and 5,000 miles by car. Gathered information, took pictures for, and wrote nearly 30 feature articles in 11 weeks. Continue to write for this magazine on a freelance basis.

PERSONAL BACKGROUND: First of three sons of design engineer. Brought up in Chicago suburb of Park Ridge. Both parents Northwestern University graduates. Attended public schools, graduating from Maine Township High School (ranked among top 10 in nation). As honor student, received special awards each year.

Commissioned Officer, U.S. Air Force, 1983-1985. In charge of writing and editorial-production work on base newspapers in three states. Received cash awards for management-efficiency suggestions. Was later promoted to office manager at S.A.C. headquarters, supervising eight men. Graduate of Air Force Effective Writing School. Honorably discharged as First Lieutenant.

PORTFOLIO OF CLIPS AVAILABLE

LOUIS KING
100 Pemberton Avenue
Boston, MA 07910
(312) 100-0000

DISPLAY DESIGN CONSULTANT
with
million-dollar record of achievement offers his talents and
services to a young, aggressive organization out to beat
competition in the display and exhibit field
by coming up with innovative ideas.

PROFESSIONAL BACKGROUND:

1983/Date - CHIEF DESIGNER, Display-O-Pack Company, Inc., an
independently operated subdivision of the General Paper Corp., a
multi-divisional corrugated manufacturer and converter.

Instrumental in organizing this division, I started with two
assistants in 1983. That year's business was $245,000. By 1985,
staff increased to 6 designers and model makers (whom I recruited
and trained), and sales rose of $650,000. At the present time,
with no appreciable increase in staff, sales for this division
have gone over the $1 million mark. Prestige of the company
enhanced through winning the Packaging Council Award, the Wolff
Award, and the Point-of-Purchase citation for creative floor
stand designs. Customer list includes Heinz, General Foods, The
Borden Company, Colgate-Palmolive, Norcross Greeting Cards.
    Phenomenal growth of business and profits attributable to
unique construction features built into design, several of which
are patented under my name. Floor stands are of one-piece
construction, easy to pack and ship, easy to assemble, and built
to carry maximum merchandise weight.
    My duties and professional experience extend beyond
planning and design. I confer regularly with sales managers,
production department personnel, and directly with clients. I am
thoroughly familiar with elements of production--from the
manufacture of the board, to printing (rubber plate engraving,
offset and silk screen), die cutting, assembly, packing, shipping
and distribution.

1978-1983 - MODEL MAKER, Sterling Mounting and Finishing Co.,
Boston, MA. Die cutters to the display field.

Work entailed planning and constructing dummies for folding
cartons and counter displays, marking out master sheets for
diecutting, folding and scoring. Organized schematic drawing
brochure showing variety of display units, tabulated by serial

number for easy identification. Mailed a promotion piece to all printers, lithographers, and silk screen processors in the New England area. The response to this promotional brochure was far more than anticipated--not merely in establishing good trade relations, but in opening 15 new accounts with a corresponding 25% increase in business. Additional publicity and business gained after parts of the brochure were reprinted (with permission) in Production Yearbook, Signs of the Times, Visual Merchandising, with a total circulation exceeding 50,000.

1975-1978 - LETTERER AND LAYOUT ARTIST, Acme Display, NY. Industrial exhibit builders.

Work entailed creating visual concepts for industrial three-dimensional displays and point-of-purchase advertising material. Personal facility in typography, hand lettering, use of jig saw, cutawl machine, air brush was fully exploited to the advantage of firm, since I was able to "pinch hit" in any of these activities which did not require the employment of specialists on a steady basis. Through personal acquaintance with promotion managers of major firms, our company was given the opportunity to bid on over $350,000 worth of window display business, the major portion of which was awarded to us because of superior design and construction. Profits rose more than 30% annually.

EDUCATIONAL BACKGROUND:

New York University, New York, NY.
        B.S. degree, 1975, Merchandising and Sales.
Parsons School of Design, New York, NY.
        Two-year Associate Degree, 1973; Graphic Design.
        (Transfer credits to New York University.)
Brooklyn Technical High School, Brooklyn, NY.
        Academic Diploma, 1971; Honor Student.

AFFILIATIONS:

Member, Point-of-Purchase Institute
Member, Art Directors Club of Boston

PERSONAL DATA:

Married; three children; wife, art instructor.

PORTFOLIO OF WORK AVAILABLE FOR REVIEW

GEORGE FONTANA
100 Macomb Road
Larchmont, N.Y. 71210
(914) 100-0000

** *:

DIRECTOR OF ADVERTISING AND MERCHANDISING

EXPERIENCE:

1986-date

National Company with distribution in mass markets. (Name withheld until job negotiations commence.)

PROMOTION MANAGER (1986-date)

Developed and executed a national promotion considered one of the best in 1988. Produced greatest in-store exposure in company's history and achieved sales objective, 35% above estimate.

Coordinated radio and point-of-purchase campaigns, local newspaper advertising and TV spots.

Produced trade ad campaigns, direct mail, brochures, exhibits and a variety of novel, creative dealer aids.

Increased distributor-paid ads for product by 300% through improved ad mat program.

Conceived an industry-wide program, endorsed by all major trade associations and written up in Sales and Merchandising magazine.

MERCHANDISING SPECIALIST (1980-1986)

Developed and managed merchandising program considered one of the most effective of its kind. Contributed to building company's stature, especially in the supermarket industry.

Produced individualized promotions for chains in support of packaged goods marketing. Sold 10 million promotion booklets a year in which chains invested over $500,000. Program produced 140 million ad impressions a year for food and packaged goods products on self-liquidating basis to company.

Assisted manufacturers and chains in solving marketing problems in connection with major promotion projects.

Wrote and made creative presentations to agencies and manufacturers resulting in 60% increase in business within a two-year period.

Developed personal contacts with top management and operating executives of leading chain and wholesale organizations. Worked closely with trade associations. Represented company at conventions, at times participated on programs as speaker or panel member.

1977-1980   **GENERAL MANAGER** - Sterling Stores, New Haven, Conn.

Planned, opened and managed new branch store. Hired and trained all personnel. Met and surpassed sales objectives through outstanding personnel and community relations in highly competitive market.

1973-1977   **BUYER, DEPARTMENT STORE** - Simon's, N.Y.

Produced consistent profit in department with recent history of losses. Increased department's volume by 50% in three branches.

1969-1973   **MERCHANDISING ASSISTANT** - T&K Company, Inc., N.Y.

Sold to department and chain stores, opening new accounts. Developed new items and merchandised new lines. Helped set up marketing plans for building a branded line.

EDUCATION:

1967-1969   **New York University School of Commerce** - Economics and Business Psychology, B.A. degree.

1965-1967   **Fashion Institute of Technology** - Merchandising and Display.

PERSONAL: Age, 43; excellent health; wife and three children; own two cars; home. Aggressive, yet diplomatic in business contacts.

Sol Brenner
100 Barnes Avenue
Brooklyn, NY 12100
(212) 100-0000

JOB OBJECTIVE:

Junior Programmer with major interest in data processing.

EDUCATION:

High School of Science, Bronx, NY; Graduate, 1984.
Drew University, Madison, NJ; B.A. (math major), 1990.

College work included:
Analytic Geometry	3 hrs.
Calculus	9 "
Advanced Calculus	3 "
Differential Equations	3 "
Theory of Equations	3 "
Functions of Complex Variables	3 "
Theory of Probability	3 "
Methods of Mathematical Statistics	3 "
Linear Algebra	3 "
Vector Analysis	3 "
Programming for Digital Computers	3 "
Physics	14 "

Technical training:
Electrical Computer Processing Institute, New York;
Intensive 10-week course in Programming for IBM 370.

EMPLOYMENT:

Worked on various part-time and summer jobs to provide 100% of my college and technical training costs. Acquired skills in typing (65 w.p.m.), operation of IBM Proof Machine, Monroe Calculator and other business machines.

MILITARY:

U.S. Army, 1984-1986. Assigned to Armed Forces Special Weapons Project at Sandia Base, New Mexico. Honorable discharge. E-5 rating.

PERSONAL:

Born 1966 - 5'8" - 152 lbs. - Single - Willing to relocate.

Carl Werner
100 Sommers Street
Washington, D.C. 20000
(617) 100-0000

COMPUTER ELECTRONICS ENGINEER

VERSATILE EXPERIENCE INCLUDES ELECTRONIC CIRCUIT DESIGN, RESEARCH AND PREPARATION OF TECHNICAL PUBLICATIONS RELATING TO ANTISUBMARINE WEAPONS PROJECTS, PREPARATION OF PROGRAMS UTILIZING AUTOCODER, IOCS FOR IBM 1440 COMPUTER.

EDUCATION: B.S. degree, Electronic Engineering and Mathematics, 1984.
University of Virginia, Charlottesville, Va.
Certificate, Engineering Administration, 1987.
George Washington University, Washington, D.C.
Certificate, Computer Programming Training Course, 1988.
International Tabulating Institute, Washington, D.C.

EXPERIENCE: PROJECT ENGINEER, Hanover Corp., Arlington, Va.
September 1988 to date.

Present work involves antisubmarine weapons equipment research for NAVSEC, Department of Navy, and technical writing on new Navy Underwater Swimmer Equipment. Wrote technical manuals on TALOS booster handling band locating fixture, revised Navy Technical Manual on hypergolic fluids, and worked on Marine Corps Technical Manual relating to mobile electric power supplies. Successfully designed and tested electrical circuit on prototype of primate food dispenser for Holloman Air Force Base.

MILITARY: 2nd Lieutenant, U.S. Army Ordnance Corps, 1984-1986.
Branch and Automotive Maintenance Army Schools (5 months); Maintenance Supervisor in repair of radio and signal equipment and weapons, small arms (6 months); Supervisor of Supply Activities (13 months).

PERSONAL: Born.................5/7/64   Health.........Excellent
Height.............. 5'11"   Marital Status....Single
Weight...........171 lbs.   Finances...In good order

Willing to relocate; U.S. Citizen; Top Secret Clearance.

MEMBERSHIP: National Society of Professional Engineers
American Institute of Electronic Engineers

GRACE JONES
100 Harrison Street
Atlanta, Georgia 01601
(316) 100-0000

COMPUTER PROGRAMMER/ANALYST

An Overview of Professional Background and Skills
(Detailed resumé and verification available on request.)

I have been in the field of computer programming for more than 15 years, during which time I have participated in the entire spectrum of systems development from analysis through design and implementation, utilizing a vast variety of hardware and software.

Hardware: IBM 30XX, 43XX, IBM System 38 & 34, IBM 370 Series, IBM PC.

Software: Cobol, RPG II, Fortran, Basic, OS/MVS, DOS, JCL Utilities, CICS, DL/I, MRP, VSAM/SPF.

EXPERIENCE:

- As **Consultant** for the past four years, have worked on a variety of projects, primarily in the area of design and installation of systems, including a major on-line manufacturing system and several financial and inventory systems. Utilized various hardware and software, among the most current being System 36, RPG II, IBM 30XX, Cobol, CICS, DL/I and MRP.

- As **Manager** for a major manufacturing company, my responsibility was two-fold:

  a) To introduce a new data processing system for a $300 million company which had no previous internal data processing capabilities. This project required the preparation of short and long-range planning, hiring of staff, improvement of internal paperwork and associated control procedures, as well as the initiation of systems development activities.

b) To establish a hardware/software planning group, which resulted in the distribution of data processing functions to various divisions, at a savings of $1.5 million per year to the company. In addition to normal project responsibilities, successfully managed a $6 million capital budget.

OTHER ASPECTS OF MY EXPERIENCE:

- Hired by a Big Eight firm as temporary Consultant and subsequently promoted to full-time Manager. Responsibilities included promoting new work, project planning and administration, staffing, supervision of design and installation, as well as billing.

- Worked for an international charge-card company in the capacity of Project Leader for the design and installation of a worldwide traveler's check sales reporting system. In addition, was instrumental in the installation of the traveler's check accounting system.

- Hired by a New York bank to design and implement a checking account reconciliation plan and a mechanized checking account balancing service to its commercial customers.

- Gave a series of advanced seminars on technical data processing.

SUMMARY:

In every case, made good use of my knowledge of systems development, methodologies and project control, capacity planning hardware and software selection, configuration, design and installation of leased switch systems.

BILL SARASOHN
100 Overbrook Drive
Hartford, Conn. 07121
(714) 100-0000

———————————— ENGINEERING ADMINISTRATION ————————————

Associated since 1974 with civil engineering and construction firms in progressively responsible administrative roles covering all operations except technical. Possess practical working knowledge in civil engineering, but forte is in management, sales, coordination of multi-project field activities operating controls, personnel, determination of policies and effective procedural implementation. Highly successful record in preparation and presentation of proposals and in maintenance of client relations. No objection to traveling, relocating.

EXPERIENCE HIGHLIGHTS

1983 to Present

Donnell Engineering Corporation, East Hartford, Conn.
Design engineers and supervisors of heavy civil engineering construction with permanent staff of up to 200.

Assistant to President

Responsibilities cover staff administration and coordination of new business activities.

Have traveled throughout Central America and the Caribbean area on promotional missions, and maintain continuing new business through personal travel and heavy correspondence.

Direct and conduct studies and projections to keep management informed on status of projects, sales prospects, projected manpower and income figures.

Prepare and present proposals for new projects based on surveys.

1979 to 1983

Roberts, Kirschner & Stoloff, Indianapolis, Ind.
Civil and structural engineers with staff of 150.

Administrative Manager

First assignment with this firm was to open, staff and manage the Paris office, to establish supervisory and inspection apparatus for $300 million U.S. Military Air Base project.

Selected and transported to Paris a group of 40 American Engineers, supported by 30 French technical and clerical personnel hired on the spot.

Appointed three key Regional Project Engineers responsible for the technical aspects of the work.

Handled personally, general administration, budgetary and other financial matters, and continuing negotiations with clients.

After this assignment (completed three months before schedule and 20% less than budget), returned to New York office.

Assisted senior partners in general reorganization of headquarters operations, formalizing policies and procedures in order to cope with rapidly expanding business. Served as coordinator (and frequent initiator) of comprehensive revisions of accounting, production and personnel.

1974 to 1979

Smithline, Robinson & Benton, Inc., Rahway, N.J.
General contractors, with permanent staff of 65.

Assistant to Vice President

Fulfilled from the beginning a varied assortment of administrative responsibilities issuing from the Vice President's office, primarily those concerned with customer relations and new business. Gradually assumed responsibility for all subcontract negotiations with building trades. Later appointed Project Manager to oversee $18 million construction project.

PERSONAL INFORMATION

Associate degree, Civil Engineering Technology, 1972 - 1974.
Mercer County Community College, Trenton, N.J. (day session)

B.A. degree, Business Administration, 1977.
Columbia University, New York, N.Y. (evening division)

Age 34; married, 3 children.

Read, speak and write French, Swedish.

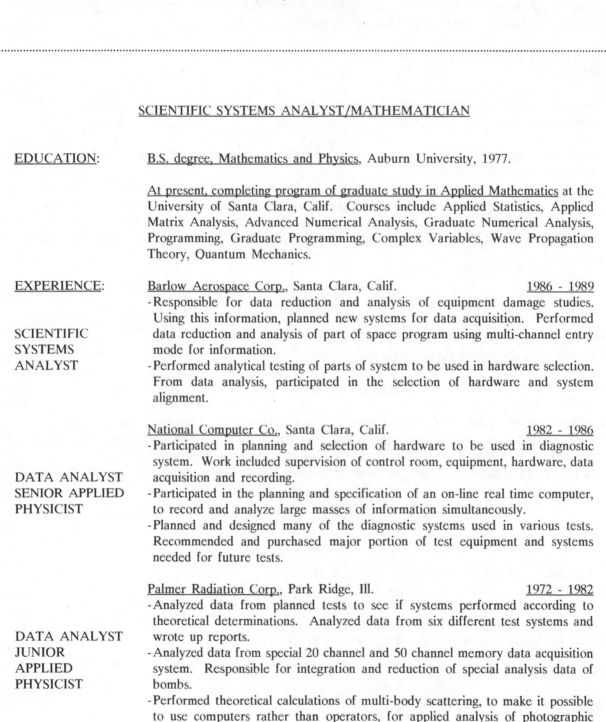

RALPH REESE
100 Leroy Street
Santa Clara, Calif. 90000
(213) 100-0000

SCIENTIFIC SYSTEMS ANALYST/MATHEMATICIAN

EDUCATION:

B.S. degree, Mathematics and Physics, Auburn University, 1977.

At present, completing program of graduate study in Applied Mathematics at the University of Santa Clara, Calif. Courses include Applied Statistics, Applied Matrix Analysis, Advanced Numerical Analysis, Graduate Numerical Analysis, Programming, Graduate Programming, Complex Variables, Wave Propagation Theory, Quantum Mechanics.

EXPERIENCE:

SCIENTIFIC
SYSTEMS
ANALYST

Barlow Aerospace Corp., Santa Clara, Calif.   1986 - 1989
- Responsible for data reduction and analysis of equipment damage studies. Using this information, planned new systems for data acquisition. Performed data reduction and analysis of part of space program using multi-channel entry mode for information.
- Performed analytical testing of parts of system to be used in hardware selection. From data analysis, participated in the selection of hardware and system alignment.

DATA ANALYST
SENIOR APPLIED
PHYSICIST

National Computer Co., Santa Clara, Calif.   1982 - 1986
- Participated in planning and selection of hardware to be used in diagnostic system. Work included supervision of control room, equipment, hardware, data acquisition and recording.
- Participated in the planning and specification of an on-line real time computer, to record and analyze large masses of information simultaneously.
- Planned and designed many of the diagnostic systems used in various tests. Recommended and purchased major portion of test equipment and systems needed for future tests.

DATA ANALYST
JUNIOR
APPLIED
PHYSICIST

Palmer Radiation Corp., Park Ridge, Ill.   1972 - 1982
- Analyzed data from planned tests to see if systems performed according to theoretical determinations. Analyzed data from six different test systems and wrote up reports.
- Analyzed data from special 20 channel and 50 channel memory data acquisition system. Responsible for integration and reduction of special analysis data of bombs.
- Performed theoretical calculations of multi-body scattering, to make it possible to use computers rather than operators, for applied analysis of photographic plates.

LOWELL NASH
100 Bergen Street
New Orleans, La. 54301
(612) 100-0000

OBJECTIVE

To acquire a position as Company Sales Engineer, mechanical or construction related, with a highly reputable firm competing in the heavy equipment market.

FORMAL
EDUCATION

M.B.A. degree, Harvard University, 1977.
B.S.M.E. degree, Ohio University, 1971.
Heavy Equipment Sales Course, Carnegie Tech., July 1981.

MILITARY
SERVICE

Captain, U.S. Army, 1971 to 1975.
Honorable discharge.

EMPLOYMENT
HISTORY

Atlas Tractor Company   Sales Engineer
New Orleans, La.   June 1983 to Present

Effected sales of tractors and other heavy equipment to commercial and residential construction firms, logging operations, mining industries, farmsteads, and the United States Government. Clientele ranged from presidents of multi-million dollar corporations to pit foremen and farm bosses. Familiar with all types of construction and heavy equipment. Increased sales in my five-state area 215% in seven years. Average annual income $91,000.

Blake-Hull Equipment Co.   Sales Representative
Baton Rouge, La.   July 1977 to June 1983

As Special Sales Representative of company, was assigned to public relations and sales of heavy equipment to all open pit mining accounts for 20 western states. Increased sales 85% in five years. Average annual income $70,000 plus bonuses.

GENERAL
INFORMATION

* Will consider relocation
* Member, National Society of Mechanical Engineers
* Pilot's License, Single and Multi-engine
* Security Clearance - Top Secret
* Income tax returns and record of sales available for review.

RON McDONALD
100 Decatur Street
Chicago, Illinois 60610
(410) 100-0000

CHEMICAL ENGINEER

SUMMARY OF
EXPERIENCE:
Background encompasses 18 years of diversified experience in the chemical industry in product management, technical sales, chemical processing, research and development. Have over three years of successful experience in selling to a variety of accounts--direct, through field outlets and brokers. Have sold to almost all levels of buying management. Have demonstrated unerring ability to forecast new buying trends, and develop new products for which there is a strong potential market.

PRODUCT
EXPERIENCE:
Hydrolyzed Vegetable Proteins, Attractants, Lecithin, Soy Flour Coatings - alkyds, epoxies, polyurethanes, butyl rubber, acrylic, silicone, polysulfide and polyester resins.

Plastisols
Adhesives - structural and non-structural
Inks and solvents
Detergents, dry starch and grocery products

BUSINESS
EXPERIENCE:
ARLINGTON MANUFACTURING COMPANY, Chicago, Ill.
Product Manager - Sales and Marketing

1983 -
Present
In my official capacity, am responsible for national territory and export items, and accountable for achieving maximum profitable sales of assigned products. Work includes planning, executing and controlling approved market programs, as well as product specifications, advertising, research and technical service, sales guidance to 24 regional and district managers. In the past three years, have guided the net profit to a 350% increase on increased tonnage of 100%.

Currently on special experimental project in Chemical Engineering Department involving chemical process work.

1980 - 1983   BAYLEY MILLS, INC. - Chemical Division, Chicago, Ill.
<u>Senior Development Chemist in Technical Service</u>

Major responsibility consisted of providing technical assistance to customers, sales staff, and production personnel. Organized technical in-service training program for sales force. Produced a 20-minute instructional film which has become an integral part of this program.

1979 - 1980   SUPERIOR PAINT AND VARNISH COMPANY, Quincy, Ill.
<u>Technical Director</u>

Responsible for development of epoxies, polyurethanes, isophthalic alkyds, and butyl rubber for finishes. Directed research and development of a new line of adhesives, plastisols and specialty compounds. The patented plastisol, specifically developed for the automobile industry, proved its superiority over competitive products. In the first six months, sales amounted to $375,000 and almost doubled at the end of the year.

1972 - 1979   PEORIA CHEMICAL COMPANY, Peoria, Ill.
<u>Product Development Engineer - Coating Section</u>

Concerned with application of silicone resins in coatings, as well as providing technical service to customers and field sales force. Recruited, trained and supervised new sales and laboratory personnel.

<u>EDUCATION</u>:   University of Cincinnati, Cincinnati, Ohio
B.S. in Chemical Engineering, 1972. Honor graduate.

Bradley University, Peoria, Illinois
Certificate, 6-month course in Advanced Paint Technology.

<u>MEMBERSHIPS</u>:   American Society of Chemical Engineers
American Chemical Society
National Association of the Paint and Chemical Industry

HENRY BERENSEN 100 Devonshire Road Pittsburgh, PA 41020 (511) 100-0000

OBJECTIVE:

Position as TOOL AND DIE MAKING ENGINEER.

EMPLOYMENT
RECORD:

TOOL ENGINEER, in charge of machine shop of a leading manufacturer of printing press equipment, located in Pittsburgh, PA.

1985/date

- Plan and design tools and special jigs needed for production and assembly.
- Consult with work supervisor in estimating time and cost of operational procedures.
- Periodically test machinery, replacing worn elements to minimize incident of breakdown during production time.
- Design many of the hand and machine tools which, prior to my association with firm, had to be imported from Germany and Sweden at great expense and often with long delays.
- Developed system of multiple die stamping which lowered labor cost by over 45% and almost doubled production output of a major unit in a screen printing press.

FOREMAN'S ASSISTANT
Richter Die Works, Inc., Milwaukee, WI.

1981/1985

- Started as Junior Die Maker and set-up man; within two years, was promoted to Foreman's Assistant. In that capacity, supervised crew of eight (all with greater seniority) with excellent managerial-staff relationship. Was selected as trouble shooter, visiting customer plants to assure proper use of dies.

EDUCATIONAL
BACKGROUND:

Tool and Die Making Apprenticeship Program
  Mechanics Institute, Richmond, VA. Certificate, 1981.
Machine Shop and Industrial Arts major
  Central High School, Milwaukee, WI. Diploma, 1978.
Home Study Correspondence Course
  Metallurgy and Heat Treatment Methods. Completed, 1984.

PERSONAL:

Age 30; born in Sweden; U.S. citizen.

Tool and die making has been a family occupation for several generations.

JEAN BAKER
000 East 68th Street
New York, NY 10000
(212) 100-0000

PHOTO

FASHION MODEL

Better-wear Dresses and Coats

PERSONAL DATA:

Age 23, attractive, well educated, single
Height: 5'6" in stockinged feet
Weight: 110 lbs. (without restraining diets)
Bust 34" Waist 24" Hips 34½"
Back to waist: 16"; excellent posture

Daughter of well-known fashion photographer.

EXPERIENCE:

MODEL, showroom and fashion shows. 1989 - Present
House of Kennington, 417 Fifth Avenue, New York, NY.
Importers of knits and manufacturers of designer dresses and coats.

SKETCH ARTIST, part-time model. 1987 - 1989
Smith & Roth, Inc., 498 Seventh Avenue, New York, NY.
Manufacturers of youthful line of ladies dresses.

EDUCATION:

Washington Irving High School, New York, NY.
Textile Design and Fashion Illustration major.
June 1985.

Endicott Junior College, Beverly, MA.
A.A. degree in Home Economics, B+ average.
June 1987.

Barbizon School of Modeling, New York, NY.
Completed 4-month evening course in Fashion Modeling.
April 1988.

INTERESTS:

Collect antiques, swimming, sewing, theater, tennis.

REFERENCES AND PORTFOLIO ON REQUEST.

THEODORE R. FORD
100 Conway Street
Akron, OH 81022
(614) 100-0000

WELDING TECHNOLOGY ENGINEER

WITH OVER 12 YEARS OF HARD CORE LABORATORY AND PRODUCTION EXPERIENCE

EXPERIENCE:

1986/date

SENIOR ENGINEER with one of country's leading producers of instantaneous facsimile duplicating devices, and pioneers in photocopying field. My responsibilities encompass:

Value Analysis: As team leader supervising staff of 28 engineers and production specialists, am in charge of evaluating reliability and cost factors of new production machines. Assignment in all phases of research and manufacturing, plus tooling and assembly production cost accounting, and inventory control. Based on last year's schedules, product savings amount of $850,000.

Advanced Fabrication Technology: Work with design and research engineers in determining feasibility of new machines and equipment, devising testing procedures for efficiency in production and service. Consult with vendors on prototype construction of machine parts.

Process Development: Review new manufacturing techniques prior to establishing technical and economic feasibility. Recommend changes when necessary.

1983/1986

LABORATORY ENGINEER, Singer Electronics, Akron, OH.
As specialist in metal joining technology, developed solderability test for printed circuit boards, acceptable by Military for inclusion in official specification standards. Served as liaison engineer and trouble shooter on metal joining and related problems in all eastern company branches. Thorough working knowledge with all forms of non-destructive testing, including ultrasonic.

1980/1983

WELDING ENGINEER, Research Division, Arco Steel Co., Detroit, MI.
Devised new methods of automatic welding operation, with saving to 25% of labor costs over previous techniques. Company expert on all welding methods -- carbon and stainless steel, especially resistance welding and tubular products.

1978/1980	**ASSISTANT RESEARCH ENGINEER**, Abbott & Wilcox, Detroit, MI. On staff of Dr. D.L. Robinson, in experimental research on welding and brazing of refractory and exotic metals (Molybdenum, Zirconium, Zircalloy, Hafnium and Beryllium) and on effect of welds on stainless steel. Developed process for brazing a spiral in boiler tubes for high temperature applications.

EDUCATION: B.S. Welding Engineering, Ohio State University, 1978.
Five-year curriculum included one year Electrical Engineering, one year Chemical Engineering, two years Mechanical Engineering, Non-destructive Testing, Corrosion Studies.

PERSONAL:

Born	3/24/56	Health	Excellent
Height	5'8"	Married	1 Child
Weight	161 lbs.	Finances	In good order

Willing to relocate.

Outstanding interests: Antiques, sculpture, ceramics.
Active sports include tennis, swimming and hunting.

MEMBERSHIP: Institute of Printed Circuits.
American Welding Society
International Association of Machinists
American Association of Welding Engineers

PUBLICATION: Commissioned by McGraw-Hill
Publishing Company to collaborate
on a textbook on welding technology.

SALARY: Negotiable.

Theodore R. Ford

WELDING TECHNOLOGY ENGINEER (page 2)

JOHN O'BRIEN   100 Greene Street   New York, N.Y. 10022   (212) 100-0000

PRIVATE INVESTIGATOR FOR LAW FIRM OR DETECTIVE AGENCY

WORK EXPERIENCE

June 1988 to Present

Municipal Police Department, Flint, Mich.

Investigate all matters involving juveniles under age of 17: interviewing, data gathering, telephone interviews, probate court attendance with juveniles in custody, preparation of cases for trial.

January to June 1988

Municipal Police Department, Detroit, Mich.

Investigate all crimes involving women of all ages and crimes committed against women by males under 17 years of age; interviewing, compiling data, observance of living conditions, preparation of cases for trial.

**Summer 1986
Summer 1987**

American Telephone Company, New York, N.Y.

As Special Services Assistant, investigated all security matters involving personnel or equipment--internal security, credit frauds, misuse of company property, preparation of cases for trial, attendance at court proceedings.

EDUCATION

School of Police Administration, Michigan University, B.S. degree in Law Enforcement, June 1988.

Relevant courses--Administrative Law Enforcement, Police Patrol Administration, Criminal Investigation, Retail Store Security, Legal Psychology, Police Science Laboratory, Criminal Law, Surveillance, Evidence and Criminal Procedure.

Franklin K. Lane High School, Brooklyn, N.Y.
Science major; graduate with honors, June 1984.

PERSONAL DATA

Age 24; single; excellent health; own car.
Hobbies - photography, swimming, karate.

MARY LEE CHIN
100 Beekman Place
New York, New York 10010
(212) 100-0000

M U S I C   T H E R A P I S T

EDUCATION: *University of Iowa*, Iowa City, Iowa
              B.S. degree, 1990. Major in music, minor in psychology.

              High School of Music and Art, New York, New York
              Diploma, 1986. Graduated top 10% of class.

              *Among college level music courses I have taken which relate to my major
              field of study, are:*
              - *Sightsinging and Dictation*
              - *Harmony and Counterpoint*
              - *Psychology of Music*
              - *Music Literature for Children*
              - *Music in Recreation and Therapy*
              - *Training in Vocal Techniques*
              - *Instrumental Musicology*
              - *American Folk Music*

              *In addition, I have had more than eight years of private instruction in
              piano, guitar, recorder and accordion.*

EXPERIENCE: *(Summers and Part-time)*

6/89 - 9/89   *Educational Alliance*, (Camp Eden) Troy, New York.
              Music Counselor for retarded children.

6/88 - 8/88   *Hilltop Country Day School*, Great Neck, New York.
              Nursery Counselor.

9/86 - 6/87   *Music Workshop*, Roslyn Heights, New York.
              Accordion Teacher, Receptionist.

6/86 - 8/86   *Henry Street Settlement House*, New York, New York.
              Volunteer Leader, Saturday Children's Trips.

PERSONAL: Date of Birth 6/26/68
              Marital Status . . . . Single
              Interests . . . . Ballet, Writing, Sports
              Languages . . . . Good command of Spanish and
                                                         Italian

John Armstrong
100 Peachtree Lane
Durham, NC 31220
(505) 100-0000

OCCUPATIONAL GOAL

RECREATION LEADER or ASSISTANT DIRECTOR: Major interest in a position in the field of recreation, with opportunity for further specialization later.

PERSONAL DATA

Date of Birth	May 21, 1968	Health	Excellent
Height	6'1"	Marital Status	Single
Weight	181 lbs.	Relocation	No problem

EDUCATION

B.S., State College at Durham, NC, 1990.
Major in Physical Education; minor in Recreation.

MAJOR COURSES

Principles, Physical Education
Individual and Dual Sports
Team Sports
Advanced Gymnastics
First Aid
Corrective Education
Aquatics (Life Saving)
Kinesiology

MINOR COURSES

Arts and Crafts
Principles of Recreation
Evaluation of Numbers
Organization and Administration
Leadership Techniques
Recreation in Hospital Setting
Community Recreation
Folk and Square Dancing

EXTRACURRICULAR ACTIVITIES

Intramural Director - Junior and Senior years.
Captain, Basketball Team - Senior year.

WORK EXPERIENCE

<u>After school hours:</u> Ass't. Director, Father Leary's Boys Club, Durham, NC.
In charge of playrooms and play areas. Coached major team sports. Taught singing games, tag games and relay activities.

<u>During summer months:</u> Ass't. Head Counselor, Topeka Hill Camp, Topeka, NC.
In charge of all games and athletic activities for youngsters in the 8-to-10-year age group. Supervised staff of nine junior counselors.

SHARON BLISS   *100 West 73rd Street*   *New York, N.Y. 10041*   *(212) 100-0000*

Licensed
DENTAL HYGIENIST

EDUCATION:

Grace Dodge Vocational High School, New York, N.Y.
Academic diploma, June 1985. Top 10% of class.
- Voted the "Girl with the Radiant smile."

New York City Community College, Brooklyn, N.Y.
Associated Degree, Dental Hygiene, June 1987.
- Active in various student organizations.

Courses included the following areas of technical study:

Oral Prophylaxis . . . . *4 hrs.*	*Oral Hygiene Practice* . . . . *12 hrs.*
Roentgenology . . . . . . *2 "*	*Periodontics* . . . . *2 "*
Pharmacology . . . . . . *2 "*	*Organic Chemistry* . . . . *4 "*
Microbiology . . . . *4 "*	*Dental Anatomy* . . . . *4 "*
Oral Pathology . . . . . *4 "*	*Preventive Dentistry* . . . . . . *4 "*

Took special course in Office Practice--typing, filing, fundamental
bookkeeping, record keeping, dental reports.

Projected educational plans: Further college work in the evening, to earn
B.S. degree.

EXPERIENCE:

Dental Assistant
Dr. Horace Larson, D.D.S., Periodontal Specialist, New York.

1987/date

- Office charge duties: Make appointments, mail checkup reminders to
patients, keep records, do typing and office bookkeeping.
- Professional duties: Assist at the chair, sterilize instruments, take and
process x-rays, mix filling compounds, prepare solutions, clean teeth.

- Reason for desiring change: Prefer to broaden my experience to
encompass general practice, eventually to work in public health or school
dental care program.

PERSONAL:

- Good speaking voice; endowed with perfect teeth.
- Like to be with people, happy disposition.
- Engaged, husband-to-be is Columbia medical student.

JEAN LUX
100 East 16th Street
New York, NY 10010
(212) 100-0000

EDUCATION:

Columbia University School of Social Work (1986, 1988)
    Graduate Seminars in Supervision
Smith College School of Social Work - M.S.W. degree (1979)
    Field work: Children's Hospital, Boston, MA
Hunter College - B.A. degree in Sociology (1978)
    Phi Beta Kappa; Student Development Committee

PROFESSIONAL EXPERIENCE:

1986 - 1988   Brooks Foster Home & Adoption Service, NY.
    Title: Casework Supervisor
    Responsibilities: Supervised five social
    workers; organized in-service training seminars.

1983 - 1986   DeWitt Children's Home, Meriden, CT.
    Title: Senior Social Worker
    Responsibilities: Casework with children and
    families; supervised student unit in social
    work.

1979 - 1983   New York University Medical Center, NY.
    Title: Caseworker, Pediatric Service
    Responsibilities: Casework, in-patient and out-
    patient pediatrics service.

PRE-PROFESSIONAL AND VOLUNTEER EXPERIENCE:

1988 - 1990   Service with Peace Corps, husband-and-wife team.
    Indian Village, Costa Rica.

1975 - 1976   Counselor, Camp Hidalgo, Bound Brook, NJ.
    Camp for underprivileged children.

MEMBERSHIP IN PROFESSIONAL ORGANIZATIONS:

    National Association of Social Workers
    American Personnel and Guidance Association

SPECIAL INTERESTS:

    Music, hiking, painting. Active in local civic
    and community affairs.

GEOLOGIST

EDUCATION
    Metro State College, Denver, Colorado
    Received a B.A. in 1982 and an A.S. in 1980.
      - Majored in Earth Science and Education.

EXPERIENCE

1988 to Present
Denver Oil & Gas Company, Lubbock, Texas
VICE PRESIDENT OF OIL AND GAS CORPORATION
Responsibilities:
- Acquiring and developing oil and gas prospects in the Appalachian Basin.

1986 to 1988
Apex Oil Company, Lubbock, Texas
AREA GEOLOGIST/GEOTHERMAL SPECIALIST
Responsibilities:
- Oil and gas leases, pre-leasing evaluations, inventory, environmental analysis, construction compliance, administration of contracts, mineral and energy resource planning in the Geysers Geothermal Field.

1984 to 1986
Geological Development Co., Denver, Colorado
PROJECT LEADER
Responsibilities:
- Involved with computer analysis and traditional geologic methods of petroleum exploration and drilling prospects.

1983 to 1984
Geological Exploration Co., Denver, Colorado
STRATIGRAPHER
Responsibilities:
- Conducted stratigraphic studies of all oil and gas prospects.
- Analysis of samples and core.

1979 to 1983
Department of Highways, Denver, Colorado
LABORATORY/TRAINING ASSISTANT
Responsibilities:
- Student teacher, mineral classification, research, training seminars for engineers.

Free to relocate to any geographic locality in the United States.

Jesse Hamilton
100 N.E. 28th Avenue #20
Hillsdale, Florida 33042
(305) 100-0000

Age: 23
Marital Status: Single
Health: Excellent

CAREER OBJECTIVE

To gain entry level position in Broadcasting, preferably in Sports.

EDUCATIONAL BACKGROUND:

1988 to 1990   Graduate ------- Florida Atlantic University
                                 Boca Raton, Florida
                                 B.A. Communications

1985 to 1988   Attended ------ St. John's University
                                 Cincinnati, Ohio
                                 Communications Arts

1981 to 1985   Graduate ------ Cypress High School
                                 Cleveland, Ohio
                                 College Prep.

EMPLOYMENT (Part-time and Summers):

Toy Town, Inc., Cleveland, Ohio - Sales Clerk, 11/82 to 12/83

Sporting Goods, Cleveland, Ohio - Sales Clerk, 6/84 to 8/85

Xavier Univ. - Games Room Supervisor, 6/87 to 8/87

Xavier Univ. - Resident Assistant, Kuhlman Hall, 9/87 to 6/88

WVXU-FM, Cincinnati, Ohio - Air-time Sales, 9/87 to 1/88

Bob Peterson Productions, 30 sec. TV Commercials - Technical and
   Production work, 4/89

EXTRACURRICULAR ACTIVITIES:

Cypress High School - Lettered in football, 1981 to 1985
                    - Yearbook Sports Editor, 1985

St. John's University - Intramural Sports, 1985 to 1987

Florida Atlantic University - Superstars, March 1989

GEORGE HARRISON
100 Bank Street
New York, NY 10012
(212) 100-0000

★ ★ ★

(Curriculum Vitae)

OBJECTIVE: PRINCIPAL or HEADMASTER of prep or military academy in New England area. Seek position in suburban school with limited student enrollment. Non-sectarian.

(Available beginning September 1990)

EDUCATION: Candidate for doctoral degree at Columbia University. Presently attending full time to complete dissertation. Expect Ed. D. to be conferred June 1990.

The City College of the State of New York, M.S., 1980.
North Texas State College, B.S., Physical Education, 1978.

PROFESSIONAL EXPERIENCE: As a licensed teacher of health education in one of New York City's junior high schools (1100 boys and girls, 12 to 15 years of age), inaugurated successful physical fitness program, which has become the model for many of the district schools, both on the junior and senior high school level. The Education page of the New York Times recently carried a feature story in praise of this program.

Introduced a highly successful series of weekly assembly programs and after-school play activities. As teacher-coordinator working in close cooperation with community groups and parent-teacher association, activated better community participation, increasing membership by 150%.

During seven-week protracted illness of regular appointed Assistant Principal, served as Acting Assistant Principal with supervisory responsibilities for 53 teachers. My duties involved supervision of instruction, orientation of the new teachers, requisition of supplies and equipment, and coordination of all faculty committees. Letters of recommendation attest to the quality of performance of these additional duties.

MILITARY: U.S. Air Force, 1972 - 1974. Separated from military with rank of Sergeant. Honorable discharge.

OUTSIDE INTERESTS: All sports, folk dancing, horseback riding, mountain climbing. Inveterate reader. Active participation in civic and community organizations.

(More detailed data available on request.)

LEO M. STEIN
100 Bay Road
Boston, Massachusetts 01460
(418) 100-0000

EDUCATION	**SUFFOLK UNIVERSITY LAW SCHOOL**, Boston, Massachusetts

J.D. expected June 1990

Honors: Isadore M. Libman Scholarship
Outstanding Young Men of America Award

Activities: Member, Real Estate Law Society
Member, Sports/Entertainment Law Society
Participant, Second Year Trial Competition
Westlaw

BOSTON UNIVERSITY, Boston, Massachusetts
College of Liberal Arts and School of Management
B.A. & B.S.B.A., *cum laude*, May 1987

Majors: Political Science & Business Administration
Cumulative G.P.A., 3.4/4.0

Honors: Golden Key National Honor Society
United States All-American Academic Award
Dean's List
Boston University Scholastic Achievement Scholarship
Connecticut Scholastic Achievement Award

Activities: Student Advisor, Collaborative Degree Program
Dormitory Representative, Student Government
Founding Member, Boston University Political Union
Captain, intramural soccer, volleyball, softball
Member, Pre-law Society
Member, Political Science Society

EMPLOYMENT

Summer 1989

Fox and Fischer, P.A., Miami, Florida
Law Clerk
Research and prepare: Settlement packages, joint venture contracts, memoranda, interrogatories, production of documents, complaints and trial preparation including findings of fact and rulings of law in the areas of: personal injury, marital, family, real property and commercial law.

June 1988 -
May 1989

Linehan, Gallagher and Mahoney, Boston, Massachusetts
Law Clerk
Research and prepare: Interrogatories, answers to interrogatories, requests for production of documents, responses to production of documents, discovery motions, third-party complaints, medical record releases, pre-trial memoranda, summary judgments, oppositions to summary judgments, conciliation appearances and trial preparation including deposition summaries, findings of fact and rulings of law.

Summers
1983 - 1987

Frank Horvath, Contractor, Connecticut
Construction Assistant
Aided in the construction of various masonry structures and conducted marketing and accounting operations.

REFERENCES Available upon request.

BROOKS ARLINGTON
100 Stuart Road
Easton, PA 61002
(512) 100-0000

PHYSICAL CHEMISTRY / ELECTRON AND LIGHT MICROSCOPY

EDUCATION:

University of California, Berkeley, CA 1984
M.S., Physical Chemistry
Lehigh University, Bethlehem, PA 1982
B.S., Chemistry and Mathematics
Rensselaer Polytechnic Institute, Troy, NY 1987
Course in Metallurgical Electron Microscopy
Northeastern University, Boston, MA 1986
Course in Metallurgical Electron Microscopy

EXPERIENCE:

ANALYTICAL CHEMIST, Chas. H. Pfizer & Co., Eaton, PA.
1984 to Present.

In charge of Electron and Light Microscopy Laboratory and Physical Testing Laboratory. Work involves selection and installation of high resolution electron microscope, scanning electron microscope, vacuum evaporator for surface replication, electron diffraction equipment and a phase contrast-interference contrast optical microscope, in addition to all supporting equipment and facilities.

With these instruments, have actively participated in the development of unusual powder metal alloys, metallic pigments, high purity metal strip, magnetic pigments, ferrites, ceramic raw materials, extender pigments and novel paper coating pigments.

ASSISTANT CHEMIST, Zenith Chemical Corp., Berkeley, CA.
1982 to 1984 (part-time).

Work involved wet and instrumental analysis of iron oxides, chromium oxides and minerals.

PROFESSIONAL AFFILIATIONS:

American Chemical Society
National Association of Physical Chemists

PERSONAL:

Age 30 - Height 6'2" - Weight 190 lbs. - Excellent health

VLADIMIR B. KAGAN
100 Evans Street
Palo Alto, California 90106

S Y N O P S I S

OPERATIONS ANALYST-ECONOMETRICIAN. Experience includes development of econometric models for management and logistic systems; economic analysis; transportation systems; coal mining electric power generation techniques; urban growth patterns; disarmament; R&D planning and long-range company resource planning.

Experience also encompasses engineering design; quality control; reliability and R&D in the field of astronautics.

EDUCATION

Ph.D. Economics, University of California, Berkeley (1977)
Fields of Specialization: Mathematical Statistics; Economic Theory; Business Cycles; Industrial Organization; Marketing.
Dissertation: The Psychology of Rationality
Honors: 4-year Fellowship in Economic Statistics (1972-1975)

B.A., School of Business Administration, Northwestern University, Evanston, Illinois (1985)
Major in business finance with minor in mathematics
Honors: Four years on Dean's list

EXPERIENCE

MEMBER OF PROFESSIONAL STAFF, Warner Electronics, Palo Alto, California (July 1985 to present)

Currently Assistant Project Leader on multi-million dollar management study of Navy Material Support Establishment. Responsible for a multi-echelon logistics support model using econometric techniques.

Other work at Warner Electronics: Econometric model of a General Electric Company component having two billion sales per year; economic analyses of U.S. railroad transportation system; coal mining; electric power generation techniques; urban growth patterns; feasible policies for adaptation to disarmament; several classified studies.

PROJECT ADMINISTRATOR, Advanced Product Planning Department, Astro-Dynamics, San Diego, California (June 1979 to July 1986)

Development of new system concepts; R&D planning; long-range company resource planning.

Other work at Astro-Dynamics: Astronautics. Progressed from Quality Control Engineer to Design Specialist; responsible for development of destructive and non-destructive test programs; experimental designs; consultation with engineering groups; development of test and reliability programs on all project proposals.

ASSISTANT PROFESSOR OF BUSINESS ADMINISTRATION, Palo Alto University, Palo Alto, California (September 1976 to June 1979)

Taught courses in Economic Statistics, Marketing, Business Policy. Consulted with various firms on such topics as: prediction of airline traffic density; retail store layout; product strategy for a small company; pricing policies.

SPECIAL LECTURER ON BUSINESS ADMINISTRATION, University of Texas, Austin, Texas (September 1975 to September 1976)

Delivered series of lectures on Marketing, Price Policies, Business Economics, Retail Store Management.

PROFESSIONAL
AFFILIATIONS

American Economic Association
Institute of Mathematical Statistics
American Mathematical Society
American Institute of Aeronautics and Astronautics

PUBLICATIONS
AND PAPERS

R&D Resource Estimation and Incentive Contracting: Some Production Function Considerations, paper presented at the Institute of Management Science National Meeting, San Francisco, 1986.

Planning a Least Cost Reliability Constrained Development Program: A Capacitated Network Approach, paper presented at First Annual Meeting, American Institute of Aeronautics and Astronautics, Washington, D.C., July 1985.

Currently collaborating on college text on Econometrics.

PERSONAL

Born August 1, 1948. Married, two children. Excellent health. U.S. citizen; top secret clearance.

SUSANNE BOYER
100 Simonson Place
Staten Island, N.Y. 10302
(212) 100-0000

EDUCATION

M.S. degree in Physiology, June 1983, University of Massachusetts
B.S. degree in Biology, June 1981, Niagara University

Undergraduate Studies	Graduate Studies
General Physiology	Mammalian Physiology
Microbiology	Endocrine Physiology
Histology	Electron Microscopy
Microtechnique	Physiological Genetics
Organic Chemistry	Microbiological Physiology
Biochemistry	Biophysics
Genetics	Special Project (involving
Cell Physiology	oculomotor physiology)
General Physics	Transplantation Immunology
Mammalian Anatomy	Statistics

WORK EXPERIENCE

Research Associate (Jan. 1986 to Present)

Neurology Department, Columbia University College of Physicians and Surgeons, New York, N.Y.

Field of Study: Muscle contraction in normal and dystrophic mice; effects of series of tetanii.

Job Duties: Use of Tektronic dual beam oscilloscopes, Grass stimulators and other electronic equipment; fine dissection work; oscilloscope trace photography; statistical evaluation of data; physiological testing on patients using Grass and Schwarzer equipment; electrophysiological recording during cryosurgery on Parkinsonians.

<u>Research Assistant</u> (Sept. 1984 to Dec. 1986)

Pathology Department, Francis Delafield Hospital, Columbia University Medical Center, New York, N.Y.

> <u>Field of Study</u>: Endocrine tumors and leukemia in rats and mice.

> <u>Job Duties</u>: Mammalian investigations including surgery, autopsy, tumor transfers, virus passage, breeding, immunoelectrophoresis and other immunochemical techniques.

<u>Graduate Teaching Assistant</u> (Sept. 1983 to June 1984)

Physiology Department, University of Massachusetts, Amherst, Mass.
Assistant to Professor Wilbur H. Brown.

> <u>Job Duties</u>: Laboratory preparation and supervision; examination, supervision and grading for introductory course in General Physiology.

PROFESSIONAL SOCIETIES

Member of:

> American Society for Physiologists
> American Association for Advancement of Sciences
> American Association of University Women

PERSONAL INFORMATION

Born: 3/16/60 in Paris, France; came to United States at age 10.
Languages: Fluent in French; working knowledge of German and Russian.
Continuing studies: Working towards my doctorate.
Hobbies: Photography, skiing, theater.
Husband: Professor of Economics, Columbia University.

Verifying credentials on hand.

ARNOLD BAKER, M.D. / 100 West 68th Street, New York, NY 10036 / (212) 100-0000

PROFESSIONAL GOAL

To participate in a program which provides good
medical care to the indigent and underprivileged.

EDUCATIONAL BACKGROUND

1974 - 1978   Columbia University, NY; B.A. degree.

1978 - 1982   Johns Hopkins School of Medicine, MD; M.D. degree.

1982 - 1983   Beth Israel Hospital, NY; Rotating Internship.

1983 - 1986   Roosevelt Hospital, NY; Three-year Residency.
                        2 years - internal medicine
                        1 year - hematology

MILITARY SERVICE

1986 - 1988   Captain, Army; Medical Corps; Fort Carson, CO.
                        Primarily in-patient service at base
                        hospital with 6 to 8 hours per week of
                        outpatient duty. Honorable discharge,
                        September 1988.

PROFESSIONAL BACKGROUND

1988 - 1989   Out-patient Clinic, ILGWU Medical Center, NY.
                        Served as examining physician for union
                        members and their dependents.

1989 - Date   U.S. Public Health Service Hospital, NY.
                        Cancer research, primarily in leukemia and
                        other related diseases.

Currently in the process of preparing for boards in internal medicine.

JOHN RICE   100 Charles Avenue   Riverdale, New York 10402   (212) 100-0000

SENIOR FINANCIAL ANALYST TO OVERSEAS-BASED COMPANY

PERSONAL: Age - 30 Height - 5'7" Weight - 150 lbs. Health - Excellent
                   Marital Status - Married, no children

EDUCATION: MBA Finance, Columbia University, New York, June 1984
                   Top quarter of class.

                   B.A. History, Wesleyan University, Connecticut, June 1982
                   Activities: Fraternity Vice President, Intramural sports.
                   Financed 50% through summer and part-time employment.
                   Linguistic abilities in French, German, Spanish, Russian.

MILITARY: LIEUTENANT, U.S. NAVY, Sept. 1984 to Sept. 1987
                   In charge of supply department (25 men) on a destroyer escort.

                   Collateral duties:
                   Financial Manager for ship. Annual operating budget totalled $410,000.
                   Inventory Manager for 18,000 different repair parts valued at over
                   $500,000.
                   Designed and implemented audit for control of financial and stock record
                   accuracy.
                   Consolidated financial and inventory management offices into one facility.

                   Several times winner of special citations.

EXPERIENCE: Continental Manufacturing Company, New York.
                   JUNIOR FINANCIAL ANALYST for eight overseas affiliates with combined
Oct. 1987   annual sales of $80 million and net profit of well over $4 million.
to Present
                   Evaluated annual and five-year profit plans. Interpreted trends of business
                   and overall market.

                   Published quarterly in-depth commentaries analyzing variances from plan
                   and last year.

                   Determined timing, content and format of profit plans, sales reports, and
                   financial statements. Co-designed standardized international reporting
                   format to be implemented shortly.

DAVE STONE
100 Rochambeau Avenue
New York, NY 10468
(212) 100-0000

OBJECTIVE   Full or part-time consultant in the field of development and production of audiovisual presentations.

EXPERIENCE   <u>1985-Date</u>   Freelance consultant for special audiovisual projects, New York City Transit Authority Training Center.

<u>1979-1985</u>   In charge of audiovisual department, Transit Authority Car Maintenance Training Center.
Trained employees in the many crafts of the transit industry, developed various types of visuals, such as viewgraphs, training books, cinema, training posters and sound synchronized slide and film strip lectures.
Researched, developed the structure and wrote the script. Did the photography, graphics and sound to complete each project.

In 1983, received a special citation and $1,000 award from the N.Y.C. Suggestion Program for the development S.O.P. Training Booklets, the use of which reduced job orientation time by more than one-third. This resulted in a saving of nearly $210,000 for the program.

Retired in 1985, after 31 years of service.

<u>1954-1979</u>   Began as a Helper in the car maintenance department of the N.Y.C. Board of Transportation (later Transit Authority). Took promotion exams and moved up to Car Inspector, Foreman, Assistant Supervisor. As Supervisor, was in charge of 60 maintainers and helpers.

Received three merit awards from the Transit Authority for improvements in processes and work techniques.

Parallel with my work at the Transit Authority, did freelance photography and experimental work in photo equipment, evenings and weekends.

Was granted several patents from the U.S. Patent Office; one of them for an automatic diaphragm control device for single lens reflex cameras. This was put into production and was written up in several photography journals.

<u>1952-1954</u> A&T Commercial Refrigeration Co., New York City. Installed and maintained refrigeration systems in display fixtures and walk-in coolers for the food industry.

<u>1944-1952</u> Eastern Golf Co., New York City.
Did bench work in the manufacture of golf balls. (Part and full time, depending on school requirements.) Helped to finance my way through schools.

EDUCATION

<u>1950-1952</u> N.Y.U. School of Engineering, with special courses in heating, ventilating and air conditioning engineering. Graduated 1954, with B.S. degree.

<u>1946-1949</u> College of the City of New York: general arts program with courses in creative writing, social science, mathematics.

SPECIAL TRAINING

<u>1980-1983</u> Completed Transit Authority-sponsored courses in: Principles of Management and Administration (N.Y.C. Board of Education); Programmed Instruction (Columbia University School of Education); Cinematography (New School for Social Research).

<u>1954-1955</u> Stuyvesant Evening High Certificate (Federal Manpower Training Program) in Machine Shop practice.

<u>1949-1950</u> Technicians Institute, New York City, Commercial Refrigeration; 1 year.

At present, attending City University towards degree in Industrial Cinematography.

PERSONAL

Born April 20, 1928; height 5'9"; weight 165 lbs.
Health - Excellent; last medical checkup in January 1990.
Marital Status - Married; three children.
Finances - Solvent; receive substantial New York City Transit Authority pension.
Interests - Jogging, painting, photography and development of instrumentation, relating to audiovisual field.

LYNN KUBAYOSHI
100 St. John's Avenue
Lakewood, N.J. 08615
(201) 100-0000

ARCHITECT

Licensed, State of New York

PROFESSIONAL SCOPE

To affiliate with innovative architectural firm specializing in the planning, designing and construction of shopping center malls in newly developing suburban communities.

EXPERIENCE

(1985 to Present) Assistant to supervising architect, Reis Associates, Lakewood, N.J., a firm employing staff of 35 which includes surveyors, team of designers, detailers, urban marketing researchers, planning architects and engineers.

My responsibilities include conferring with clients, recommending designs to meet their specific requirements; document study of zoning laws and building codes, assist in coordinating work of planning architects and staff engineers; oversee constructing, coordinating efforts of team of four junior architects.

(1983 to 1985) Staff architect, Lane Associates, New York, N.Y.

Served as liaison with architects, designers, management consultants, and construction engineers. Was co-recipient of Architectural League's annual award for outstanding work of young architects and designers.

PROFESSIONAL TRAINING

Columbia University, School of Architecture, 5 year course, B.S. 1983.
Mechanics Institute, evening course in structural design (at present).

PERSONAL

Age: . . . . 29 **Height:** 5'3" **Weight:** 114 lbs. **Health:** Excellent
Marital Status: . . Married, husband is freelance package designer.
Finances: . . . . . . Good, live within my means, no outstanding debts.
Rent 6-room house, own car and station wagon.

PROFESSIONAL AFFILIATIONS

Member:
* American Institute of Architects
* National Association of Interior Designers
* Architectural League of New York

PHIL ORLANDO
100 Green Street
Chicago, IL 72205
(706) 100-0000

PHOTOCOMPOSITION SUPERVISOR

EMPLOYMENT HISTORY

8/87 - present

Paccaro Corp., Chicago, IL
Computerized typesetting house

PRODUCTION COORDINATOR/PLANNER. In the main, duties entail typographic makeup of college and technical texts, following client specifications; overseeing the work through inputting, computer composition, typesetting, proofreading and correction cycles. Responsible for the total production of any given text. Utilize IBM 370/135, OS multiprogram environment and a Harris Fototronic photocomposer. Familiar with latest computer word processing developments.

6/85 - 8/87

Graphics, Inc., Chicago, IL
Computerized Phototypesetters

SUPERVISOR OF COMPUTER OPERATIONS. Duties entailed scheduling and running an IBM 360/40, DOS, single partition computer and an RCA Videocomp 800 photocomposer, coordinating the various aspects of page makeup, programming, correction cycles, data manipulations and photocomposing. Also, analyzing data for programming--i.e. for fielding, edit insert, etc., as well as designing and implementing forms for tape logs, production controls and job run sheets.
   Was originally hired to set up and supervise the Proofreading Department. After becoming familiarized with the computerization aspect of cold type production, was promoted to position of Formatter with substantial increase in salary.

9/84 - 6/85

Daily Press, Chicago, IL
Newspaper Publication

EDITORIAL ASSISTANT. Worked as proofreader on the lobster shift, while in my junior and senior years at Chicago Tech. Acquired a working knowledge of the fundamentals of photocomposition.

EDUCATION

Hold B.A. degree in English Literature, Chicago Tech, June 1985.
Completed Systems Analysis Course, Merrill School, 1986.

PERSONAL NOTE

Married - one child; four brothers in family, all in printing field.

SELF-APPRAISAL PERSONALITY RATING SCALE

*How do you see yourself objectively in relation to
the requirements of your particular career goal?*

	POOR	FAIR	MED.	GOOD	EXC.
How do I rate in general appearance?					
To what extent am I tactful and diplomatic?					
Am I a good listener? To what extent?					
Am I a self-starter? To what extent?					
How do I rate myself in native intelligence?					
Am I inclined to see the other person's point of view?					
Am I innovative and creative?					
Am I generally easy to get along with?					
How good is my memory for names and faces?					
How do I rate in ability to express myself clearly?					
Do I get bored doing the same work for an extended period of time?					
Do I make friends easily?					
Am I more of a leader than a follower?					
To what extent do I have a definite career goal?					
How do I rate myself in quality of speech?					
Do I react well to adverse criticism and benefit by it?					
Do I have a happy disposition?					
Do I have the innate ability to size up a situation clearly?					
Am I endowed with an analytical mind?					
To what extent do I have control over my temper when I am crossed?					
Am I well adjusted emotionally?					
Am I generally inclined to be enthusiastic?					
Do I show patience for work involving detail?					
Am I a well-organized individual?					
Do I like to be with people?					
How do I rate myself scholastically?					

THE JOB INTERVIEW

MEETING YOUR PROSPECTIVE EMPLOYER

You can consider your résumé as having fulfilled its purpose if as a result of it you have been called for an interview. Hardly ever—it would perhaps be more accurate to say *never*—is anyone hired for a responsible position without a face-to-face meeting with a prospective employer who will want to see at first hand how you, the applicant, measure up in relation to the credentials indicated on your résumé.

What the interviewer is interested in at this stage is not merely the hard facts, but in addition, an overall evaluation of you as a person—your general appearance, grooming, manner of speaking, attitude, tact and other subtle characteristics that show you to be the kind of person who is trustworthy, cooperative, ambitious and easy to get along with. To sum it up, are you likely to be an asset to the company?

A job interview can be a tense if not traumatic experience. More so, if you have not gone through it a number of times before and are unprepared to engage in a dialogue and successfully field the questions that may come up during the course of the interview.

100 Questions most frequently asked by the interviewer

The number of questions, as well as their sequence, will naturally depend upon the kind of position you are being interviewed for and the direction the interview takes.

1. Tell me what you know about our company and its position in the industry.
2. In what ways will our company gain by hiring you?
3. How does your work and education experience help to qualify you for the job on hand?
4. If you are currently working, why do you want to switch jobs at this time?
5. Your résumé indicated that all the jobs you have held have been only for a short duration. Why?
6. How long do you plan to stay with our company?
7. How would you define your long-range goals and career objectives?
8. Would you be able to work overtime on occasion, if needed?
9. Would it be feasible for you to relocate to one of our branches in another city if that proved necessary?
10. How do you respond to criticism?
11. How do you spend your vacation and spare time?
12. Briefly, what are your financial status and obligations at the present time?
13. How did your previous employer treat you?
14. How did you secure your previous job?
15. Were you ever dismissed from a job for a reason that seemed to you unjustified? If so, tell me something about it.
16. Have you other job offers you are considering now, and on what basis would you select this job rather than the others?
17. Because of the security nature of the position, it is our policy to require a

prospective employee to submit to a polygraph test. Would you agree to such a test?

18. Do you consider yourself a natural leader or are you inclined to be more of a loyal follower?

19. Looking back, what is the worst thing that has happened to you? What is the best?

20. What do people think of you? In your opinion, do they size you up correctly?

21. How is it that you are unemployed at present?

22. Do you have any mixed emotions about working for a person considerably younger than you are, or for a woman supervisor?

23. How do you cope under pressure?

24. What are your major strengths and how have you capitalized on them?

25. What do you consider to be your major weaknesses and how have they affected your work, life and general attitude?

26. Does your present employer know that you are looking for another job?

27. When you consider your total employment history, what type of work did you enjoy the most? Which least?

28. As you grew up, what have you contributed towards your family finances, or your own schooling? Are you still doing it?

29. Have you been able to maintain a systematic savings program through planned budgeting?

30. What courses in school did you find exciting and most beneficial? Which bored you and were a waste of time?

31. Based on your knowledge of the field, who would you say are our chief competitors?

32. In what ways are you active in community work, social, fraternal, civic or other organizations?

33. Which of the previous firms you worked for did you like the best? Why are you no longer there?

34. Not all of us are blessed with a happy home life. How has yours been up to now?

35. Your résumé shows that you've been with one firm for a long time without any appreciable increase in rank or salary. Why didn't you venture forth to seek a job with better prospects?

36. You state on your résumé that your health is excellent. When was your last physical checkup?

37. At present our firm is faced with the following problem which relates to your field of specialization. (Brief explanation of problem.) What could you hope to contribute to help solve it?

38. Let's assume hypothetically that you consider your supervisor unfair or difficult to work with. What would you do about it?

39. Are you easily ruffled when things don't go your way?

40. Have you ever dropped out of school before getting a diploma or degree? If so, why? Do you regret it?

41. Are you prepared to work full time, or are you interested in seasonal or part-time employment?

42. Do you have any physical or emotional condition which might interfere with your performance on the job?

43. Do you have patience for detail, routine work, problem solving?

44. In your opinion, what is necessary to succeed on a job or in business?

45. Do you have any difficulty in making decisions for fear of coming up with the wrong one?

46. Are you taking any courses for self-improvement or college credit? Do you plan to do so in the future?

47. What professional associations or

trade journals help keep you abreast of developments in your field?

48. It's been said that it's not *what* you know, but *who* you know that really counts. How do you feel about that?

49. If a job were offered you, who would make the decision to accept it? You alone, or with your spouse jointly, or anyone else?

50. Do you have friends or relations working for our company?

51. What suggestion or innovation of yours on your previous jobs were adopted and turned out to be of benefit to the company?

52. Looking ahead, what position do you hope to hold with this company some years from now?

53. What was the salary progress on your previous job?

54. What type of people attract you? What kind do you shy away from?

55. Under the *Personal* heading of your résumé, you state that you are divorced. At the present time, do you feel up to it to talk about it?

56. Do you consider yourself a well-organized person?

57. Do you work well as a member of a team or are you more comfortable working independently?

58. Do you recall the most difficult work assignment you ever tackled? How did it turn out?

59. Why are you changing careers at this time in your work history?

60. Have you ever been in conflict with the law except for such minor offenses as traffic violations, speeding, illegal parking, etc? Have you ever been convicted of a major offense? If so, explain.

61. As a department supervisor what procedure would you follow in recommending the dismissal of a worker who has proven to be inadequate on the job?

62. Why would you like to work for this company?

63. Would you be willing to take calculated risks when necessary?

64. I'd be interested in knowing what rubs you the wrong way.

65. During your school or college days, were you ever elected an officer or leader in any social, athletic or scholastic organization?

66. Are you at the present time under the care of a physician or other medical person? If so, what is the nature of that care or treatment?

67. In the last twelve months, how much time have you lost from school or work, and for what reason?

68. Have you ever held a position of trust, handled money or confidential material? Have you ever been bonded?

69. If you are not a U.S. citizen, do you have the legal right to work in this country?

70. At the present time, are you in the habit of taking narcotics or other hard drugs without a doctor's prescription?

71. Have you ever worked for this company before under another name?

72. Have you served in the armed forces? If so, what was your branch and rank? Are you currently in the reserves?

73. Do you understand that a condition of employment with our company requires a medical checkup conducted by a physician of our choosing?

74. Do you hold a driver's license? Has it ever been revoked? Is it now restored? What was the reason for the revocation?

75. Succinctly, tell me the story of your life, highlighting those aspects which made you what you are today.

76. As a boss or supervisor, would it bother you to fire an incompetent worker or would you keep him (or her) on, making fewer demands on him because you

know he needs the job?

77. Have you ever been fired or requested to resign? What were the circumstances as you remember them?

78. What do you do to keep in good physical condition?

79. Why is it that you are not making more money at your stage of life?

80. Who would you say has had the greatest influence on your life?

81. There seems to be a number of unexplained gaps in your employment history. Would you explain the reason for these?

82. Before coming to a decision to hire you, what references should we *not* follow up at this time? Why?

83. What was your starting and highest salary on your last job?

84. What salary do you expect with us?

85. What attributes do you look for in a friend?

86. In your opinion, what personal qualities make for an ideal supervisor or boss?

87. What does it take to make you happy?

88. Can you tell us something about your family?

89. What is the nature of the occasional criticism that your employer or supervisor made about your work? Can you relate specific examples?

90. What do you do for relaxation?

91. Do you own life insurance, a car or home?

92. Do you have any outstanding debts at the present time?

93. Are you generally inclined to hold center stage in a group or organization?

94. What personal sacrifices are you prepared to make to succeed on the job?

95. If we hire you, when can you start?

96. What supplementary income, if any, do you have?

97. What was your scholastic average in high school? In college?

98. How good is your memory for names and faces?

99. Location-wise, would you encounter any problem getting to work on time and maintaining a good attendance?

100. Are there any questions pertaining to the job in particular, or about the company in general, that *you* would like to ask *me*?

Questions you may ask the interviewer

Here is a sampling of the type of questions that you can safely ask the interviewer without appearing to be overly aggressive or inquisitive. In fact, most interviewers will consider such questions a favorable indication of your interest in the job.

In an extended interview it is customary for the person who interviews you to mention the company's policy in reference to such things as fringe benefits, pension plans, basis for salary increases, promotions, etc. Should these or other points of information not be touched upon or explained sufficiently, it is your privilege to bring them up as the occasion arises.

• Is this a permanent job, or of a temporary or seasonal nature?

• What is the company's policy in regard to promotion from within the ranks?

• Can you tell me something about the company's pension and retirement plans, hospitalization and insurance coverage for employees and their families?

• Does the company have a set salary schedule for the various job classifications?

• Are salary increases based on merit alone, promotional exams or length of service?

- How long has my predecessor in this position been with the company and why is he no longer here?
- Would it be feasible for me to take a short escorted tour to meet the people I will work with?
- Do you have a stock-sharing plan in which employees of the company can participate?
- If my job requires the use of a car, will the company supply me with one, or help defray the cost of maintaining it?
- If I am hired as a department supervisor, how many people are in my department and how long have they been there?
- Is membership in a trade or professional union a prerequisite for employment with this company?
- If for any reason my professional credentials do not match the requirements of the position with this company, is there any other company you know of that I might contact?
- How soon after the interview will I know whether I am hired?

INTERVIEW PITFALLS AND HOW TO AVOID THEM

Some time ago a survey was made by the Director of Placement at Northwestern University to determine the common causes of failure in job interview situations. From actual records of interviews submitted by the personnel directors of over 150 large corporations, a list of 50 reasons was compiled. This list appeared in a very informative job-guidance booklet published under the auspices of the New York Life Insurance Company. Some of the most prevalent causes of failure indicated in the survey are listed here, with suggestions for eliminating them.

Poor personal appearance

You can't very well help it if nature has not endowed you with the handsome features and perfect figure of a popular movie star, but you *can* improve your grooming and neatness of appearance. Employment counselors agree that good grooming, appropriate dress, and care in body hygiene are major factors which consciously or subconsciously influence the prospective employer's personal reaction to the applicant.

Overbearing, overaggressive, conceited, superiority complex— "know-it-all" attitude

The interviewer is likely to respond negatively to the applicant who displays an arrogant "know-it-all" attitude. A confident, optimistic attitude is fine, but don't act the part of the pushy supersalesman. Let your record or samples of work speak for you.

Inability to express oneself clearly —poor voice, diction, grammar

Some authors of job-guidance books recommend that applicants take extensive speech lessons and put in hours of daily practice in speech drills; but, under the circumstances, that is unrealistic advice. When you are busy job hunting, you can hardly be expected to have the time or the patience for elocution lessons. However, you *can* try to be more mindful of the way you speak. Get someone to listen to you who will point out shortcomings in your speech pattern, or listen to a playback of your voice on a recorder to help you improve your enunciation and diction.

Your general speech pattern will be helped immeasurably if you are well-prepared with ready answers to questions likely to come up during the interview.

Lack of planning for a career; no purpose or goal

The interviewer is bound to get an unfavorable impression of you if you have no clear idea of the kind of job you are looking for. If you say, "I can do anything," you reveal by your alleged versatility a lack of a specific objective. The interviewer will respect you more if you state in specific terms what you are capable of doing, and how it ties in with your long-range career goal.

Lack of confidence and poise, nervousness

Excessive nervousness and lack of confidence are deeply rooted emotional traits that even psychiatrists find difficult to correct. You can, however, make these personality shortcomings less noticeable by adequate preparations. This means preparing a well-organized résumé and thoroughly familiarizing yourself with it, as well as with answers to questions that the interviewer is likely to ask. Good grooming and proper dress also appreciably contribute to a feeling of confidence and poise.

Overemphasis on money

Don't give the impression that a big paycheck is your main interest and that it constitutes the only reason for your desire to work for the company. In your interview you will ultimately discuss salary, but you should do so discreetly by equating it with more cogent reasons for your interest in the job.

Poor scholastic standing—just got by

If you have not distinguished yourself scholastically, don't apologize for your educational shortcomings, but rather emphasize what you are doing at this time to correct them. Tell what you are doing to upgrade your education—courses you are taking or plan to take, professional affiliations, cultural pursuits, etc.

Lack of courtesy—ill-mannered

Social amenities are as important in business as they are in personal relationships. "Thanks" and "please" are words easily found in the dictionary, but not used often enough. An interviewer instinctively is antagonistic to an applicant who shows poor manners or lack of courtesy.

Your general attitude and behavior are indicative of your personality and character. Most job counselors agree that good personal attributes are in many ways as important as technical proficiency. Some say they are even more so.

Failure to look interviewer in the eye

Strange, isn't it, that this should be listed as a common reason why some applicants fail the interview? Nonetheless it is true that the interviewer is inclined to have a vague distrust of an applicant who consistently evades his glance. He is left with the impression that the applicant is either not straightforward or, at best, is extremely shy and insecure.

When you are seated opposite the interviewer—or are involved in any two-way communication—put your "best face forward." Register interest in the conversation by directing your remarks and your gaze at the interviewer, not at the floor or ceiling, and listening intently in turn. Make the interviewer the center of your interest and attention.

Limp, fishy handshake

There is something about a limp, fishy handshake which suggests a lack of moral stamina. If the interviewer extends a hand, accept it as a gesture of good will and friendship. Respond with a firm grasp of your full hand, not merely your fingertips. But don't overdo the hearty handshake bit, by being a bonecrusher or handpumper.

Unhappy home life

If you are unhappy at home, can't get along with your parents, have been the victim of marital conflict, or have had a nervous breakdown, don't tell your interviewer all about it at the very first meeting. Such a background may mark you as a potential "security risk," someone with unresolved problems that may interfere with your duties on the job. If you aren't blessed with a happy personal life, don't bring up the subject, but if the interviewer does, then, of course, answer all questions honestly but without elaboration.

Sloppy application blank

An application blank with crossed-out writing, missing information, smudges, or fingerprints obviously militates against anyone applying for a position as accountant, secretary, commercial artist, or other occupations where accuracy and neatness are requisite work traits. But neatness and accuracy are important to vary-ing degrees for *any* responsible position, and the appearance of your completed application serves as a graphic sampling of those attributes. The same thing also applies to the appearance of your résumé.

Job-hopping

Interviewers watch for symptoms of instability in the job applicant's history. If you have had a succession of short-duration jobs, it would seem to indicate that you do not know what type of work you want to do, that you lack persistence, or worse still, that you might have been dismissed from the multiple jobs you have held.

If, by chance or choice, you have had a number of short-duration jobs, don't elaborate on this phase of your work-experience record and erroneously identify yourself as a chronic job-hopper.

Cynical outlook

It is one of the interviewer's responsibilities to the employer to screen out the cynical applicant. A cynic can easily become a malcontent, and that is one step away from a trouble maker. Obviously such a person is no asset to any company.

Take the chip off your shoulder when you go for a job interview.

Inability to take criticism

There are times on the job when you may be subject to criticism (sometimes even unjustly) by your superiors or co-workers. The ability to take criticism and benefit by it is a desirable attribute. To test that ability, prior to employment, an interviewer may try to throw you off guard by some remark deliberately intended to rub you the wrong way. Don't let a discussion turn into an argument, even if you are right. It takes moral fortitude to present a point of view, but it takes diplomacy and tact to avoid an argument.

Late to the interview

"But I thought the interview was for 12:30 not 11:30." ... "I took the wrong train." ... "I had to wait for a cab in this rainy weather." ... "I forgot my portfolio and halfway down here turned back home to get it." Any excuse for lateness to an interview, even a valid one, starts you off on the wrong foot. You begin the interview on the defensive.

As a safeguard against lateness, start out early enough to allow for unforeseen delays en route. If you find that you have arrived at your destination early, you can always use the spare time to good advantage. It gives you an opportunity to stop for a cup of coffee or a smoke, and to freshen up a bit. It also gives you a chance to review your résumé and your "sales pitch."

Failure to express appreciation for the interviewer's time

The good impression you make on an interviewer can be hurt if you leave the interview without acknowledging appreciation for the courtesy extended to you. If you think you did well on the interview, clinch it not merely with verbal thanks, but by following it up with a short, thank-you note. And even if you feel that you somehow failed to make a favorable impression, write a thank-you note anyway. It may help to turn the tide in your favor, especially if the correspondence includes some additional evidence of your qualifications not brought out in the interview.

Your letter may read something like this:

Dear _____:

Thank you so much for the time spent in interviewing me for the job as Comptometer Operator. As it may be of interest to you to see the letter of commendation I spoke of, I have taken the liberty of enclosing a copy of it.

You know how very much I would like to be associated with your company and how hopefully I anticipate a chance to work for you in the near future.

Sincerely yours,

DOS AND DON'TS FOR JOB INTERVIEWS

1. Don't look annoyed if you have to wait beyond the time scheduled for your interview. Instead, keep yourself profitably occupied by reviewing your résumé or other aspects of your job presentation.

2. Don't enter the interviewer's office wearing a top coat. It's better to carry it neatly folded over your arm or leave it in the waiting room. Wearing a coat during an interview conveys the impression that you can stay only momentarily and have more pressing business elsewhere.

3. Don't begin the interview with a negative remark, such as, "It's sure stuffy in here," or, "This is certainly a difficult place to get to," or some other personal observation which may put your interviewer on the defensive. Instead, begin on the positive side, even if it is not more than a complimentary remark about the attractive décor of the waiting room or the pleasant and courteous manner of the receptionist.

4. When entering the interviewer's office, don't sit down until you are invited to do so.

5. It's a friendly gesture to shake hands, but it's best to wait for the interviewer to make the first move. It's the interviewer's prerogative to initiate this token of cordiality.

6. Don't place your portfolio, package, purse, or anything else on the interviewer's desk unless you first ask for permission to do so.

7. Try to fix the interviewer's name in your mind, and use it occasionally during the conversation. Everybody likes to hear the sound of his or her own name. Don't you?

8. Put your best face forward—and that's the face with a friendly smile. A friendly smile turns strangers into friends.

9. Don't chew gum during the interview. It indicates a lack of sophistication—and also interferes with clear speech.

10. Make it a point to look at the interviewer as you speak or listen. Meet him or her eye-to-eye. An evasive look bespeaks a lack of straightforwardness or excessive shyness.

11. Avoid expressions like "frankly speaking" or "to tell you the truth" or "to be perfectly honest with you." These phrases, in effect, imply that you aren't always frank or truthful.

12. Speak distinctly. Don't mumble under your breath.

13. Don't give excuses for past failures. Answer all questions honestly and show how you have actually benefited by some of your previous mistakes.

14. Be modest in your claims; let the achievements recorded in your samples or résumé speak for you. Nobody likes a braggart.

15. In presenting a portfolio as a visual part of your "sales pitch," let the interviewer set the pace in examining the contents. You must assume that the person who looks through the portfolio is quick of mind and eye and knows what to look for. If the interviewer fails to look at every one of your samples, don't say, "But you haven't seen this yet." Your samples should be clearly marked, making it unnecessary for you to keep up a running commentary.

16. "Don't smoke during an interview" is generally a good rule to follow. But if you are an inveterate smoker, and you are offered a cigarette, you may accept. Even with the interviewer's invitation to smoke, avoid lighting up one cigarette after another. Excessive smoking shows that you are tense. Don't advertise it!

17. Don't "knock" your previous employers or go into a detailed account of your gripes and grievances. There is nothing to be gained by it. Speaking against others in no way enhances your own position.

18. Don't try to ingratiate yourself by betraying confidences or revealing trade secrets of your previous employers. There is no surer way to convince the interviewer that you can't be trusted.

19. Don't listen or appear to be eavesdropping on telephone calls which may temporarily interrupt the interview. You can make discreet use of this interlude by taking note of awards, certificates or other documents or pictures proudly displayed in the office. Your observations can be the subject for some complimentary remarks when the interview resumes.

20. Remember to leave a copy of your résumé with the interviewer, even if you are not specifically requested to do so.

21. Sense when the interview is over. It's easy to tell. You'll get the cue when the interviewer rises as if ready to escort you to the door, or starts thanking you for "coming in," or begins to shuffle through some papers as if ready to resume some

prior, unfinished business. Don't overstay your welcome. Leave while you're ahead!

22. Make it a point to thank the interviewer in person as well as with a follow-up note. It is advisable to forward a brief, but well-worded thank-you note for the courtesy extended to you during the interview. It also affords you the opportunity to allude to some favorable aspect of your discussion and helps to reinforce the good impression you have made.

ANNOTATED BIBLIOGRAPHY SELECTED WITH A VIEW OF BROADENING YOUR SCOPE OF THE TOTAL JOB MARKET

What Color Is Your Parachute? Richard Nelson Bolles, Ten Speed Press, 1990

Don't be confused by the rather obtuse title; the subtitle, "A Practical Manual for Job Hunters and Career Changers," helps to clarify the objective and contents. This book has been an all-time best-seller in its field for good reason. The author strongly advocates ways and means by which the job seeker can undertake a planned and well-coordinated job-search campaign on his or her own, without resorting to expensive job-search firms— and come out the better for it. Mr. Bolles is refreshingly outspoken in his assertions, witty and charismatic. He has had the courage to shake up many traditional concepts of job hunting techniques.

Sweaty Palms, H. Anthony Medley, Lifetime Learning Publications, 1978

A once-over-lightly treatment of how the average job applicant feels and fares in an interview situation, and what the applicant can do to successfully survive this experience. Based on the author's long professional experience, it is replete with numerous case histories.

The Professional Job Changing System, Robert Jameson Gerberg, Performance Dynamics, 1980

A hard-cover book presenting many valuable ideas for job hunters interested in positions on the professional, managerial and executive levels. A handbook for finding a job with a future, it has been well received in the field.

How to Win Friends and Influence People Dale Carnegie, Simon & Schuster, 1964

A timeless treasure trove for those who seek practical guidance on how to get along with people and get them to like you. This is a practical must-read book on human relations which has sold millions of copies and undoubtedly will never go out of print. Chock-full of case histories and true-to-life anecdotes. By all means, read this book from cover to cover and re-read it at intervals to keep the advice it contains foremost in your mind at all times.

Getting a Job After 50, John S. Morgan, TAB Books, Inc., 1990

If you think you're over the hill and too old for the job market, this is a good source of information and inspiration.

Where the Jobs Are: A Comprehensive Directory of 1,200 Journals Listing Career Opportunities, Dr. S. Norman Feingold and Dr. Glenda Ann Hansard-Winkler, Garrett Park Press, 1989

This books lists where jobs are advertised in hundreds of career fields. A comprehensive index helps job seekers to locate periodicals most likely to offer help.

How to Write Your First Professional Résumé, J. I. Biegeleisen, Perigee, 1986

A practical guidebook intended for those about to enter or re-enter the job market, with sample résumés to go by.

110

Robert Half Way to Get Hired in Today's Job Market, Robert Half, Rawson Wade, 1983

An authoritative and practical guide written by an outstanding personality in the field of employment.

Jobs '90, Kathryn and Ross Petras, Prentice Hall, 1990

Serves as a directory of the faster-growing companies and covers more than 20 different industries.

Jobs—What They Are, Where They Are, What They Pay, Robert O. Snelling, Sr., and Anne M. Snelling, Simon & Schuster, 1989

Written with authority by the founders of Snelling & Snelling, one of the world's largest employment agencies. Deals with careers in many lines of work and how to prepare for them.

Dress for Success, John T. Molloy, Warner Books, 1988

Emphasizes the importance of appropriate dress for business and industry, and is applicable for those seeking high-level positions in the job market.

Get a Better Job, Ed Rushlaw, Peterson's Guides, 1990

A general guide for searching and finding a job that's right for you.

REFERENCE DIRECTORIES FOR CONTACTING BUSINESS FIRMS AS PART OF AN ONGOING JOB SEARCH CAMPAIGN

Standard & Poor's Register of Corporations, Directors and Executives, published annually by Standard and Poor

This three-volume directory has an alphabetical listing of approximately 37,000 corporations. Gives names, titles, functions, and phone numbers of almost 390,000 officers and other principals.

Dun & Bradstreet Million Dollar Directory, published annually by Dun & Bradstreet

Contains a listing of firms with a net worth in excess of one million dollars. Lists large corporations alphabetically, geographically and by product classification.

Thomas Register of American Manufacturers, published annually by Thomas Publishing

A nationwide advertising directory alphabetically listing thousands of business firms, showing products, addresses, and services, as well as names of major officers and their titles.

Encyclopaedia of Associations, published by Gale Research Company

A compendium of major trade and professional associations throughout the United States. Brochures issued by various associations are available on request.

College Placement Annual, published by the College Placement Council, Inc.

This publication is especially useful to recent college graduates preparing to enter the job market. Emphasis is on firms interested in recruiting young college graduates. It lists specific job areas of employment, whom to contact, addresses.

To a large extent, your success in getting the job that's right for you depends not only on your résumé (as important as that is), but on your perseverance in all phases of your total job-search campaign—and a lot of good luck!

J. I. Biegeleisen

111

PERIGEE'S PRACTICAL HANDBOOK SERIES

__**THE ART OF LETTER WRITING**
by Lassor A. Blumenthal   0-399-51174-1/$8.95
A sensible, highly effective guide to dispel the anxiety involved in putting pen to paper,
it offers concrete hints on creating memorable letters for all occasions.

__**JOB RÉSUMÉS (REVISED EDITION)**
by J. I. Biegeleisen   0-399-51692-1/$7.95
Completely revised and updated, this valuable resource offers the most thorough
selection of samples available and will help job hunters easily write eye-catching
résumés.

__**SHORTCUTS TO INCREASE YOUR TYPING SPEED**
by Elza Dinwiddie-Boyd   0-399-51489-9/$8.95
Whether for a typewriter, computer or word processor, this book is a groundbreaking
guide to increased typing speed.

__**SUCCESSFUL BUSINESS WRITING**
by Lassor A. Blumenthal   0-399-51146-6/$8.95
How to write organized and effective letters, proposals, résumés and speeches that
bring surefire success to any business situation.

__**TOUCH TYPING IN TEN LESSONS**
by Ruth Ben'Ary   0-399-51529-1/$8.95
The shortest complete home-study course that covers all the fundamental skills of
touch typing. This classic handbook has taught the basics of typing to more than a
million people.

__**TYPING FOR BEGINNERS**
by Betty Owen   0-399-51147-4/$8.95
Newly updated, this is the standard basic manual for mastering the keyboard. Includes
self-teaching and learn-at-your-own-speed methods.

__**TYPING MADE EASY**
by Elza Dinwiddie-Boyd   0-399-51671-9/$8.95
This Practical Handbook manual can teach anyone how to type in only ten days using
the proven "See It, Say It, Strike It" method.

Payable in U.S. funds. No cash orders accepted. Postage & handling: $1.75 for one book, 75¢ for each additional. Maximum postage $5.50. Prices, postage and
handling charges may change without notice. Visa, Amex, MasterCard call 1-800-788-6262, ext. 1, refer to ad # 584c

Or, check above books and send this order form to: The Berkley Publishing Group 390 Murray Hill Pkwy., Dept. B East Rutherford, NJ 07073 Please allow 6 weeks for delivery.	Bill my: ☐ Visa ☐ MasterCard ☐ Amex _____ (expires) Card#_____ ($15 minimum) Signature_____ Or enclosed is my: ☐ check ☐ money order	
Name_____	Book Total	$_____
Address_____	Postage & Handling	$_____
City_____	Applicable Sales Tax (NY, NJ, PA, CA, GST Can.)	$_____
State/ZIP_____	Total Amount Due	$_____